THE ART OF

MARZIPAN MODELING

THE ART OF

MARZIPAN MODELING

Casey Sinkeldam

VNR VAN NOSTRAND REINHOLD
New York

Library of Congress Catalog Number
ISBN 0-442-23957-2

Printed in the United States of America

Van Nostrand Reinhold
115 Fifth Avenue
New York, New York 10003

Chapman and Hall
2–6 Boundary Row
London SE1 8HN, England

Thomas Nelson Australia
102 Dodds Street
South Melbourne 3205, Victoria, Australia

Nelson Canada
1120 Birchmount Road
Scarborough, Ontario M1K 5G4, Canada

16   15   14   13   12   11   10   9   8   7   6   5   4   3   2   1

Library of Congress Cataloging-in-Publication Data

Sinkeldam, Casey
    The art of marzipan modeling / by Casey Sinkeldam.
        p.   cm.
    ISBN 0-442-23957-2
    1. Marzipan.   I. Title.
TX791.S55   1991   90-12161
641.8′65—dc20   CIP

FOREWORD

This book, which devotes itself to the history and production of marzipan, covers all aspects from the cultivation of almonds through the creation of numerous marzipan modeling projects, from simple figures to complex scenes. It could not have been written at a more appropriate time and certainly not by a more qualified author.

Complete with 134 black and white instructional photographs and an 8-page color photo insert, Casey Sinkeldam shares with the readers his philosophy and experience spanning nearly a half century of work as one of the most notable pastry chefs in this country. The work itself should thoroughly familiarize the reader with all the basic techniques and specialized skills that a successful pastry chef should acquire.

Casey Sinkeldam's credentials are virtually unsurpassed and his skills as pastry chef on numerous Olympic teams have always added that extra special touch of quality to the U.S. teams. As a pioneer in his field, and one of the truly great pastry chefs, Casey Sinkeldam's influence has added to the interest, awareness, and appreciation of fine pastries, and has helped raise the level of the profession in this country.

This comprehensive work on the art of marzipan modeling should become an integral part of every institutional and individual library serving the serious food professional.

Ferdinand E. Metz
President, The Culinary Institute of America

PREFACE

DEVELOPING YOUR TALENT

Without question, working with marzipan, as with any other culinary craft, can be rewarding, not only financially, but also in terms of giving enormous personal satisfaction and a feeling of accomplishment. Some people were born with the desire to create and knew it when young; for others it developed as a hobby or as some related special interest grew. Regardless of its origin, it is important to pursue it. How do you start? I suggest the following: Learn to look. You can see beautiful lines, curves, and design in buildings, churches, cathedrals—everywhere. Go to art shows and museums. Even a trip to the corner drugstore to look at birthday, anniversary, and special event greeting cards can provide inspiration. The point is to learn from the ideas and talents expressed by professionals and then synthesize these to create your own.

I highly recommend that you attend or participate in culinary food shows. The creation of artistic food and pastry showpieces for exhibit is an excellent way to give everyone—students, apprentices, and professionals—the chance to learn as well as to exhibit one's work. For those who are just beginning, it is a way to create an awareness of your shortcomings. For those with experience, it is a place to receive recognition for your talents and efforts. Everyone who participates in a food show increases his or her knowledge. When you go, take pictures, ask questions, make notes. Otherwise, you will forget. Whenever possible, try to talk with the professional, the medal winner, or the master. It is always best to learn from an expert, whatever the field. In other words, go for the best and always ask yourself, "What new thing did I learn that I didn't know before?" This is the only way to develop one's potential.

The food industry is constantly changing, and going to a culinary show is also an excellent way to stay current. What is good today could be out of date tomorrow. Taste and color preferences, portion control, new ingredients and equipment, and nutritional guidelines are shifting and changing continually. Without exposing yourself to a forum where new ideas can be exchanged, you will surely relegate your knowledge and skills to obsolescence.

In the end, however, it is an old story. There is yet no school or method whereby you can speed up the acquisition of practical experience. The only way is to practice freely and experiment making new forms. Sometimes the results are daring, be they successful or not.

My hobbies are oil painting, clay sculpture, watercolor, and making stained glass. With each new interest, I have gone to school and learned from a professional teacher. Even if your interest is not in art, you will be surprised what you can learn about proportion, color, and shape that can be applied to your culinary craft.

Don't waste your time and mind! We can all learn. Today, more than ever, the opportunities are great. The industry needs creative and innovative individuals. You can give that knowledge. It will give you great returns.

Casey Sinkeldam

ACKNOWLEDGMENTS

I wish to thank the individuals who have contributed their knowledge and expertise to make this book useful. I am grateful to master pastry chef Jan Weetink of the Netherlands for being my good friend for almost 40 years. I promised him that I would show some of his talents in this book. I am also grateful to Susan Brauner, director of communications at Blue Diamond, for providing me with information about the history, cultivation, and production of almonds as well as almond paste for modeling many of the figures. Thanks are also due to Snyder Photography Inc. and Doré Studios for the fine pictures.

Most of all, thanks to my wife Cora and daughter Patty for their support. I dedicate this book to them.

CONTENTS

INTRODUCTION

This book contains step-by-step instructions for both students and professionals who want to learn about modeling with marzipan. It represents more than 40 years of experience in the food industry, of which much time was spent judging food shows. By providing such a guide, I hope to spark interest and creativity in this and in all aspects of the culinary arts. I hope it will be useful not only to those who want to teach themselves, but also to those who will instruct and guide others.

The instructional portion of this book, the first five chapters, is based on my research and on the techniques that I have shown at seminars. During these seminars, most people could make a simple figure after one or two demonstrations. After reading the first part of this book, I think you will be able to do this as well. My approach is to keep the method as simple as possible while still retaining the figure's appeal in its final form. As an orientation, I have also included two chapters about almond cultivation and the history of marzipan.

The second half contains examples of decorated cakes, showpieces, and displays made exclusively with marzipan, as well as pieces made with a combination of marzipan, plastic or modeling chocolate, pastillage, and royal icing. The purpose of these examples and the accompanying instructions for more advanced techniques is to show the virtually limitless range of possibilities—from the simplest to the most complex—that are achievable using these versatile, edible decorations.

THE ART OF

MARZIPAN MODELING

ABOUT ALMONDS

A BRIEF HISTORY

Although we do not know exactly where almonds originated, or who first
cultivated them for use as a food, flavoring, or for their lovely, light oil, we do
know that almonds were grown long before the Christian era in Greece, in
Anatolia (the western part of Asia, comprising nearly all of Turkey), and
throughout the Middle East and southwestern Asia. Most authorities agree
that almonds and dates, both mentioned frequently in the Old Testament,
were among the earliest cultivated food plants.

Records tell us that almonds were well established in Greece in ancient
times. In a history of plants written about 300 years before the time of Christ,
Theophrastus, a Greek scholar, mentions the almond tree as the only one in
Greece that produced blossoms before leaves. Their first recorded appearance
in the kitchen was in 400 B.C. when an enterprising Anatolian cook combined
them with meat.

The Romans brought almonds to Italy from Greece around 200 B.C., calling
them "Greek nuts," where they were welcomed enthusiastically as a taste treat to
enjoy or in combination with other ingredients, especially in the form of sweets.
In fact, almonds coated with sugar (known to us today as Jordan almonds) first
appeared in the Italian diet in 177 B.C. The introduction of "Greek nuts"
to Egypt and a number of western European countries, as far north as
England, is directly linked to the expansion of the Roman Empire.

Italian merchants also transported the culinary technique of using ground
or pulverized almonds as thickener (popular in Middle Eastern cuisines) to

countries north and west of their homeland. Crusaders of the eleventh, twelfth, and thirteenth centuries, upon returning to northwestern Europe, played a major role in popularizing the use of ground almonds for thickening and flavoring.

The invasions of the nomads into settled societies reached their height with the great Mongol invasions of western Asia and Europe in the thirteenth, fourteenth, and fifteenth centuries, particularly under the leadership of Genghis Khan. The nomads originated a nutritious confection similar to the high-energy fruit and nut bars carried in backpacks by mountain climbers and hikers today.

The Moors were originally the inhabitants of Mauritania, a country that encompassed large portions of what is now northern Morocco and western Algeria. Like the Arabs, they made extensive use of almonds in their cuisine in both sweet and savory dishes. The vast groves of almond trees in Portugal's southernmost province, Algarve, and along the Levante coast of Spain were originally planted by the Moors.

During the 500 years of Moorish rule, the Court of Madrid became the most elegant in all of Europe. The excellence of its cuisine was matched only by achievements in the arts and sciences. The Moors incorporated the technical cooking skills and creativity of the Persians and Arabs; the ancient knowledge of the Egyptians; the citrus, almonds, and other fruits of the Greeks; and spices from the East. Their cuisine was a wonderfully rich, exotic, and spicy blending of ingredients that has been passed down to this day.

From Spain, almonds traveled abroad with New World explorers to Mexico. In the middle 1700s, the Franciscan Padres brought almond trees to California via Mexico, in order to grace their missions along El Camino Real, the main road that stretches all along the coast from San Diego to Sonoma. However, these trees died after the missions were abandoned. The next attempt at growing almonds in the United States was in 1840, when some trees imported from Europe were planted in the New England states. The climate was too severe there, and the attempt was not successful. In time, plantings were made down the length of the Atlantic seaboard and into the Gulf states. But the almond's exacting climatic requirements ruled it out as a profitable crop in these areas.

By the 1870s, research and cross-breeding had developed several of today's prominent almond varieties. By the turn of the century the almond industry was firmly established in California, where ideal conditions for growing almonds were found in the Sacramento and San Joaquin areas of the state's great Central Valley. Today, California is the only place in North America where almonds are grown commercially, and their yield represents over half of the world's supply. The balance is grown in Italy, Sicily, Spain, Majorca, and other European countries.

CULTIVATION AND PRODUCTION

Almonds are a member of the rose family and are botanically related to apricots, cherries, peaches, and plums. The propagation of almond trees is interesting. Peach rootstock is used in most orchards because of its disease resistance and early production. Peach pits are closely planted in nurseries, and after about eight months, the sweet almond bud is budded onto the young peach seedling. From the time of planting, it takes approximately four years before the trees begin to bear fruit, and another four years for a tree to reach its prime.

Almond cultivation in California is centered in the state's sunny inland valleys, where brief winters provide a necessary period of dormancy for the trees. Spring comes early in these areas, bringing ideal warmth in February and March for the emerging almond blossoms. Although spring frosts are an annual threat, sprinklers and wind machines help protect orchards against unexpected cold snaps.

In the summer the trees are watered through regular sprinkling or by flooding the orchards several times during the growing season. The number of leaves on the trees is said to give some indication of the crop, the idea being that the fewer the leaves, the greater the room for fruit.

During August, the outer hulls begin to open along the trees' branches, revealing the tan-shelled almonds inside. As the crop matures, the hull, shell, and kernel dry out, and the skin of the kernel turns brown. As the nuts dry, they become easier to remove and tend to fall. Harvest times vary from year to year and from district to district, but usually begin in August or early September.

At harvest time, hydraulic shakers are moved in to grip the trees' trunks, shaking the branches until the almonds fall to the ground. The crop is then gathered by mechanical harvesters, and the hulls are separated from the almonds by hulling equipment before delivery to the processing plant. The hulls are an important by-product, providing several hundred thousand tons of valuable cattle feed annually.

When the almonds arrive in the factory, they are weighed, graded, and cleaned. Later, many of the almonds are blanched by special machinery, the sole purpose of which is to remove the brown outer skin. They are also processed into ground almonds or into various types of fancy cuts, such as split, sliced, and slivered, or sold in their original form as whole natural almonds. It takes approximately 2 pounds (900 grams) of unshelled almonds to produce 1 pound (450 grams) of kernels.

CHAPTER 7

ABOUT MARZIPAN

THE MARZIPAN TRADITION

Marzipan, a confection of ground almonds and sugar, is impressive, delicious, and easy to work with. Because of its texture and malleability, it can be fashioned into whatever imagination and dexterity dictate—fruit for center-pieces, bouquets of flowers, miniature objects for displays, and figures and buildings for historical tableaux. Of course, it has many culinary applications as well, such as garnishes for pastry, fillings for fruits and nuts, centers for chocolates, and coatings for cakes and petits fours. It is also served as a traditional holiday treat in many countries.

Almonds have long been used in cooking, but when they were first crushed and sweetened to form what is now known as marzipan is un-clear. The combination is believed to have originated in the Middle East, where it was discovered by the Crusaders, who brought it back to Europe. There are at least two stories as to how it became popularized in Europe. One story relates that the Ursuline order of nuns at Issoudun in France first developed it as a candy, where its fame spread across Europe and as far as Russia. Another story is that it was invented in Italy during a grain shortage, when finely ground almonds and sugar were kneaded together to form an unbaked sweet "bread." Even the word "marzipan" itself is open to conjecture. Marzipan, or *massepain*, an old term for it in French, may be derived from the Italian word *marzapane*, which originally meant "sweet box" and later what it contained. Or perhaps it comes from *marci panis*, Latin for St. Mark's bread, which is what marzipan is called in Venice, the city whose patron saint is St. Mark.

It is recorded, however, that as early as 1368, the Holy Roman Emperor Charles IV received gifts of lovely gilded loaves of *marzapane*. Pope Pius V served pears wrapped in it, and Vienna's Emperor Franz I enjoyed it filled with nougat cream. A popular after-dinner amusement in elegant circles was the presentation of allegorical pageants modeled with marzipan figures.

Elizabeth I liked her "marchpane," as it was called in England, on a round wafer frosted with sugar and rose water. Always a favorite in the Tudor and Stuart courts, plain marzipan was made into flat cakes and cookies and molded into ornamental forms. What was known as royal marzipan was fashioned into rings and wreaths, dipped in marmalade, egg white, and powdered sugar, and baked until puffy. After the mid-1700s, it was usually made into fruit shapes, with the exception of the traditional English wedding and Christmas cakes—dark, dense fruitcakes covered with a layer of the almond and sugar paste and finished with hard royal icing.

In thirteenth-century France, marzipan was made with pistachios as well as with almonds. Today, French pastry shops sell almond paste in fruit and vegetable shapes, and Aix-en-Provence has a famous diamond-shaped specialty moistened with orange-flower water on a brittle wafer base. Caramel-covered prunes filled with marzipan, and walnut halves sandwiched together with the confection and dipped in caramel appear during the holidays.

Marzipan came to the New World with the European colonists. Dutch immigrants brought generations-old wooden marzipan molds when they settled in Pennsylvania, and replaced them when they wore out with ones made by local craftsmen. The colonists also modeled the paste by hand.

A Holiday Specialty

German children say that the best marzipan arrives on the Christmas platter, served in some families on December 6, the feast of Santa Claus, or on Christmas Eve, along with the presents. The platter is heaped high with brightly colored fruits, cookies, "potatoes" rolled in cinnamon, and "sausages"—all made from marzipan.

Danes give one another *marcipan* pigs for good luck. In early December, friends get together to form the candy into decorations for the tree. In Spain, *melindres de Yepes* are marzipan treats glazed with egg white, lemon juice, and sugar, and dusted with powered sugar.

MAKING MARZIPAN

Marzipan is made by adding sugar and corn syrup or glucose to almond paste (approximately 1 part almonds to 2 parts sugar plus glucose) to make the mixture pliable, smooth, and easy to roll or mold. Almond paste itself is a finely ground paste of ground blanched almonds and sugar (although some brands contain corn syrup or glucose as well). Often used in fillings for pastries and coffee cakes, it is usually less sweet, is stiffer, and generally has a coarser texture than marzipan. Marzipan should be finer, smoother, and more elastic than almond paste. The terminology can be confusing, especially since in the United States, unlike in France, there are no recognized guidelines defining the amount of sugar to nuts, which, depending on the brand, can vary from 25 to 50 percent sugar. The greater the percentage of almonds, the better the flavor—and the higher the price.

Almond paste can be made from scratch, but few people do this any-more—including myself—since it is inefficient given the easy availability and high quality of commercially prepared products. Both domestic and imported almond pastes are available through wholesale suppliers, mail-order cata-logues, and some supermarkets. I am told that the French almond paste labeled *pâte d'amandes fondante* or *confiseur* can be used for modeling without adding sugar, but I have not tried it myself. I used Blue Diamond almond paste, bought in seven-pound cans, to make the marzipan for all the decorations and figures in this book. It has an excellent taste with a good, pliable texture.

Before You Begin

When you work with marzipan, you must take extra care to ensure absolute cleanliness at all times. Never let marzipan come into contact with flour or yeast. This can be dangerous as it may cause the marzipan to ferment. If you work in a bakery, do not shape the marzipan on any surface or table that has been used for doughs as it may harbor yeast spores. I recommend that you use a marble or Teflon surface that can be easily cleaned and sanitized.

Before you begin, remove any rings and scrub your hands and fingernails. Wear clean and dust-free clothing. Remember that you are working with a product that people can eat, and it is necessary to observe strict hygiene.

Use a clean and sanitized stainless steel bowl and mixing paddle or hook when mixing the marzipan. Other kinds of materials could cause a discolora-tion. Any modeling tools, knives, or other equipment that you use must be scrubbed and sanitized before you begin.

7

The Recipes

Any of the three following recipes can be used for making marzipan for modeling. Choose the one appropriate for your needs and taste; each formula will make a very presentable product. I prefer to use the first recipe made with corn syrup. The second recipe with fondant works well too, particularly if you need a very white mixture and a silky texture. Although you can make fondant from scratch (consult any good pastry or baking cookbook for detailed instructions), commercially prepared fondant works fine here too—I use it. The third recipe with gum tragacanth (a jellying agent available at baking supply shops) is good if you prefer a more "rubbery" texture.

The sweetness and texture of marzipan can be controlled by the amount of powdered sugar added. If the marzipan is to be used for decoration only, add more sugar to stiffen it. If it is to be eaten as part of a cookie or cake, use less. Corn syrup or fondant is added to make the mixture more malleable; the powdered sugar is incorporated to make it stiff enough to shape. Note that metric conversions have been based on 28 grams per ounce (the exact equivalent is 28.35 grams).

MARZIPAN I

	Amount	Procedure
Almond Paste	10 ounces (280 grams)	In a mixer blend the almond paste and corn syrup until it forms a smooth
Corn Syrup	3 ounces (84 grams)	paste. Add enough powdered sugar to make the marzipan stiff enough to
Sifted Powdered Sugar	12–15 ounces (336–420 grams)	shape.

MARZIPAN II

	Amount	Procedure
Almond Paste	24 ounces (672 grams)	In a mixer blend the almond paste and the fondant until it forms a smooth
Fondant	10 ounces (280 grams)	paste. Add enough powdered sugar to make the marzipan stiff enough to
Sifted Powdered Sugar	16–18 ounces (448–504 grams)	shape.

MARZIPAN III

	Amount	Procedure
Sifted Powdered Sugar	2 tablespoons (28 grams)	In a small bowl mix the powdered sugar with the gum tragacanth. Add the water and mix thoroughly. In a mixer blend the almond paste and the gum tragacanth mixture until it is lump-free and smooth. Add enough powdered sugar to make the marzipan stiff enough to shape.
Gum Tragacanth	1 tablespoon (14 grams)	
Cold Water	2 ounces (60 ml)	
Almond Paste	15 ounces (420 grams)	
Sifted Powdered Sugar	16–18 ounces (448–504 grams)	

After you have mixed the marzipan, let it stand at room temperature for 24 to 36 hours before you use it. This will allow the oil from the almonds to be reabsorbed and the marzipan to firm up. Place it in a plastic bag sealed airtight and put the bag in a covered container. If it is exposed to air for too long, the marzipan will form a crust, which must then be cut off before it is used.

Flavoring Marzipan

Usually, additional flavorings are added to marzipan only when it is used in making cookies, candy, or cakes. In those cases, the flavor can be enhanced by adding nuts, chopped candied fruit, mocha, chocolate, or liqueurs. When marzipan decorations are meant for display and not for consumption, flavoring them is superfluous. If the marzipan is to be used as a cake or candy filling, it can be softened by adding simple syrup until it has reached the desired consistency.

COLORING MARZIPAN

For good results and eye appeal, color is as important as shape. Color can be kneaded into the marzipan before it is formed, or sprayed or brushed on afterward, or both. Liquid, paste, or powdered food colors can be used. If you use a liquid, it is important that the color be strong enough. Adding too much liquid to achieve the right shade will over-soften the texture. Always use good, new government-approved food colors; older colors could have lost some of their potency.

Unless you are coloring a very small amount, take approximately one-quarter of the total marzipan to be tinted and slowly add enough food color, noting how much you use, until you are satisfied with the shade. Calculate how much you will need for the whole, and knead it into the rest of the marzipan. By working with a small amount at first, you will avoid ruining a whole batch of marzipan if you make a mistake with the color.

Generally, marzipan looks best when it is tinted with pastel colors rather then with dark, muddy ones. Brown, however, is a color that is often used, particularly for animal figures. Although you can certainly use a brown food color, tinting the marzipan with a paste made from cocoa powder mixed with corn syrup and a little red food color produces an excellent deep chocolate-brown shade.

Spraying

Applying color by spraying it on with a spray gun, atomizer, or air brush is a very effective way to create depth and shade gradations not possible by just tinting the marzipan alone. The color is made by diluting food color in alcohol or water. Alcohol is best because it evaporates and dries quickly, minimizing the chance that the color will drip, and since it dries so fast, it is good to use on humid days. You can use any inexpensive whiskey, gin, or vodka. Although you can use paste, powder, or liquid food color, I prefer to use a liquid because it is easier to dilute.

For best results, place the food color in a small container. If you use a powder, make a soft paste with a little liquid to completely dissolve the particles. If you use a paste, soften it also with a little liquid. I usually use a plastic spoon for mixing. Before you dilute it for the spray, be sure that the color particles are completely dissolved. If they are not dissolved, the particles can spot and then bleed and spread over the marzipan as well as block the nozzle of the spray gun.

Add enough alcohol or water until the desired color has been reached, and fill the spray gun. Always test the color on a piece of white paper before you begin to spray the marzipan. If it is too strong, add more alcohol; if too weak, add more food color. Any extra diluted color can be stored in a plastic bottle for use next time.

Spraying Technique

Hold the spray gun, atomizer, or air brush about 20 inches (50 cm) from the marzipan to be sprayed. If you hold the gun any closer, the droplets will disperse unevenly and the marzipan will get too wet. You can control the effect by the angle you hold the spray gun. Holding the gun at 45 degrees, 60 degrees, and at eye level to the object will change the color density. Spray back and forth in one direction, and you will soon notice how the highlights of the object stand out. You can apply several coats over your base color as long as those colors complement each other. When spraying fruits, for example, a fine mist of light brown over a base of white or light yellow will give the surface definition and depth. Just be sure to let each coat dry between applications.

STORAGE

Marzipan and almond paste have a high percentage of sugar and a low moisture content. This makes the growth of bacteria low, almost impossible. With proper handling, marzipan can be stored for several months before it is formed, as long as it is protected from drying out. Keep it tightly wrapped in plastic and stored in a covered container at room temperature. Avoid refrigerating it, since excessive moisture can create mold and cause the surface to "sweat." Marzipan, however, like most foods, tastes better and is easier to work with when fresh.

If the marzipan is to be eaten, it is best to do so when it is fresh and in optimum condition, just as you would want any cake or cookie to be. Although it will depend on the size of the decoration, generally marzipan will remain soft and edible for two weeks, provided it has been protected from drying out with a thin coating of cocoa butter (see next paragraph) and stored in a dust-free environment at room temperature. At the very least, however, let a new marzipan decoration rest overnight at room temperature before placing it on a cake or cookie. A thin crust will form, which will give the figure some support.

I recommend that you spray or brush a marzipan decoration with a thin coat of fresh cocoa butter (applying too thick a coating with give a "soapy" taste). This will keep the marzipan from drying out as well as give it an attractive, glossy sheen. Melt the cocoa butter and apply it with a soft brush or use a spray gun. There are edible lacquers available which are used for candies that would serve the same purpose, but I prefer cocoa butter because it is a natural product and tastes better.

If you plan to keep the modeled marzipan indefinitely (as for a centerpiece or display piece that you plan to exhibit again), store it in an airtight plastic container or box to prevent insect contamination. It is a good idea to reduce the humidity in the storage box by inserting a dessicant such as Humisorb. For additional protection, but *only* for those pieces that are strictly for display, you can spray the surface with a plastic lacquer. Note, however, that permanent fixatives are not permissible if you plan to enter the piece in a food show.

CHAPTER 3

MODELING

DEVELOPING A STYLE

Modeling is a creative art form, be the medium clay or marzipan. The reproduction of natural beauty has always been a fascinating subject, as history has shown. Over the years, new materials have been developed and discovered, and the modeler has adapted a style and approach to accurately reflect the times in which he or she lived. When marzipan became a popular item on the gourmet table in Victorian times, the confectioner or pastry chef was quick to use it as a modeling medium.

Starting with simple shapes formed from marzipan pressed in carved wooden molds, people began to use marzipan to replicate popular shapes, such as pets and figures. Pastry chefs, as culinary craftsmen, developed more complicated designs, although marzipan was largely reserved as a decoration for cookies, cakes, and candies. A variety of styles emerged—some good and some leaving much to the imagination.

In the 1920s, modeling was influenced by a fresh new concept. It was in this decade that a gentleman by the name of Walt Disney made his debut with a style that was to have an impact on the whole world. He devised a characterization in its most appealing form—the world of fantasy. Because of the influence of this great man's genius, modeling styles took a turn for the better, especially for confectioners and pastry chefs—and especially for me.

I believe that everyone has his or her own style, and that is good. In this chapter I will show you how to make the basic shapes and how to hold them together. The next three chapters will describe how to form small figures, flowers, and fruits using these basic shapes. These pieces were developed using my own style; you must practice, practice, practice to develop your own.

MODELING TOOLS

modeling sticks	grater
scissors	screen
metal cutters	plastic scraper
ribbed rolling pins	marble slab
smooth rolling pin	spray gun
ruler	powdered sugar
small knife	foam rubber
small spatula	plastic spoon
sieve	sponge with egg white

Figure 3-1 is a photograph of the tools and equipment I used in producing the marzipan decorations I created for this book. Most of what you may need can be easily purchased in any kitchen or baking supply store if you don't own it already.

Scissors   A small pair of scissors is useful for clipping a piece of marzipan to separate ears or legs or to make delicate decorative cuts. Scissors are also used to form flowers such as the narcissus or daisy.

3-1

Modeling sticks   These can be purchased in any crafts or art supply shop. Modeling sticks are useful, but certainly not mandatory, and a simple plastic spoon will often do as well (see below). The following three sticks are the ones I use most often:

1. A stick with a large rounded bulb at one end and a small rounded bulb at the other. This is good for making eye sockets on animals and figures and for forming shallow rounded cavities and indentations.
2. A stick with a sharp point. This stick can be used to make small holes such as for nostrils or a mouth.
3. A flat stick, like a tapered tongue depressor, that comes to a point at the broad end. By turning this stick on its side and using the sharp end, I can, for example, mark lines to define toes, claws, or fingers or trace a hip bone on an animal's haunch. It's also useful for scoring lines, such as veins on a flower leaf.

Metal cutters   A set of metal cutters can be used for cutting out uniformly shaped leaves or petals.

Ribbed rolling pins   These special wooden pastry pins are used to roll out uniform decorative patterns. The two pins pictured and used for this book create a raised waffle pattern and a ribbed ribbon design.

Ruler   The ruler is used for production. It is a fast way to measure the amount of marzipan you will need when making multiples of the same figure. For example, assume you need to make ten figures composed of three pieces of marzipan each. The three pieces weigh 1 ounce (28 grams), ½ ounce (14 grams), and ¼ ounce (7 grams), or a total of 1¾ ounces (49 grams). First, make three 10-inch (25-cm) long rolls of marzipan weighing 10 ounces (280 grams), 5 ounces (140 grams), and 2½ ounces (70 grams) in the proper colors. Then place the rolls against the ruler and cut 1-inch (2.5-cm) pieces. You will have 30 pieces sized correctly, or enough to make ten figures.

Small knife   This simple tool is used for cutting or for making fine incisions. It can also be used for scoring lines.

Small metal spatula   This useful tool is used to lift pieces of marzipan, without bending them, off a work surface.

Sieve   I use a sieve for dusting powdered sugar over some marzipan fruits to create a slightly "fuzzy" appearance.

Grater   By lightly pressing a piece of marzipan fruit between two graters while rolling them gently, you can create a bumpy pitted pattern.

Screen   A screen is used for dispersing food color over a surface. By dipping a toothbrush in food color and rubbing it over a screen, you can get a very natural-looking spotty effect or a soft blush when coloring fruits, for example.

Plastic scraper   A plastic scraper is useful for smoothing and thinning the edges of marzipan when making flower petals. If you don't have a plastic scraper, the bowl of a plastic spoon will also work.

Marble slab   This is my preferred counter surface when working with marzipan since it stays cool and is easy to clean. Other appropriate surfaces are Teflon-coated and formica counters. Avoid wood counters because they are hard to keep clean and can harbor yeast spores that could contaminate the marzipan.

Fixative gun   This sprayer, or any other simple spray gun or atomizer, is used to apply a mist of food color over a marzipan object to create additional depth and dimension. Sprayers can range from simple plastic spray guns, like the kind you would fill with cleaning solution to wash windows, to sophisticated air guns pastry chefs use in bakeries to decorate cakes. If you are planning on using this only occasionally, buy something inexpensive. Just make sure that the mist can be adjusted to a fine spray.

Powdered sugar   Powdered sugar, confectioner's sugar, or 10X sugar, whatever you prefer to call it, is used to keep marzipan from sticking to the work surface or to your hands. Use it sparingly, though. Too much can affect the taste, and if it is adheres too heavily to the surface, it can dull the finish.

Foam rubber   A small piece of foam rubber is useful for supporting a modeled marzipan figure or flower until it dries enough to support its own weight.

Plastic spoon   This is my favorite tool, and everyone who attends my teaching seminars notices this. The handle end can be used to poke holes; the bowl can be used to smooth out edges or held vertically as a knife to indent lines.

Sponge with egg whites   I use egg whites as an edible glue to stick pieces of marzipan together. An easy way to apply it without getting it on your fingers is to soak a clean sponge in a small dish of whites. Dab the piece of marzipan right on the sponge.

This list is only a suggestion. Improvise with what you have. I have seen people extremely well equipped with all sorts of tools and supplies who still cannot produce. Use what is available, and don't forget that the best tool of all is your clean hands, which can fashion most of the figures and flowers in this book.

BASIC MODELING SHAPES

Most of the figures described in this book are based on three basic shapes: the ball, the pear, and the sausage. The ball is the most basic, because no matter what the shape, you must always begin with a ball. Most forms are shaped in your hands—not on the table. If the marzipan seems too soft, add some powdered sugar, but do so sparingly since it affects the flavor. If the marzipan is too stiff, add a little corn syrup. You want to keep the texture firm enough to hold its shape, but not overly dry so that it becomes brittle. If the marzipan is too soft, it will droop.

When rolling the marzipan on the table, either to form it into a sausage or to roll it out to cut, dust the surface with a little powdered sugar to keep it from sticking. You can also dust your hands with some powdered sugar, if you like, but this is not necessary.

Ball (Fig. 3-2)   To make a perfect ball, roll the marzipan between the palms of your hands, just as you would a meatball, until it is perfectly smooth and completely seamless. A round shape can only be achieved with your hands, so don't roll it on the table.

Pear (Fig. 3-3)   Make a perfect ball, and by slowly rolling and pressing with the palms of your hands, push out a rounded point, like the neck of a pear.

Sausage (Fig. 3-4)   Make a perfect ball and roll the marzipan on the work surface using the palms of your hands, pressing slightly with your fingers until the marzipan forms a sausage or log shape. Many figures are made by tapering one or both ends of the sausage so that the center is thicker than the ends.

3-2

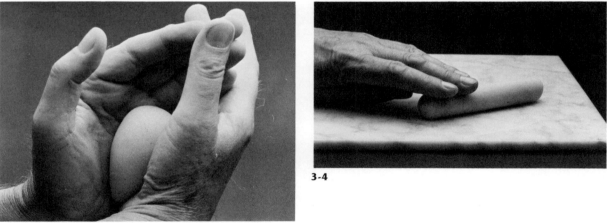

3-3

3-4

Learn these three shapes before you go on to two more useful forms: the bean and the curve.

Bean (Fig. 3-5)   The bean shape is used for making figures such as a dog or a cat, or for making a baby face. Make a ball and then a short sausage. Place it in one hand. With the other hand, press one finger in the center, and by gently rolling and pressing slightly, form a slight curve, keeping an equal thickness on both ends. The center of the bean should be slightly thinner than the ends.

Curve (Fig. 3-6) The curve shape is useful for forming a goose or swan neck or an elephant's trunk. Make a ball and then a pear. Place your hands in a praying position, fingertips together, with the neck of the pear down, toward your wrists. Apply pressure downward with your palms, and roll the pear slightly to extrude the neck. The more you roll, the thinner and longer the curve will be. A goose neck would be quite thin, an elephant's trunk bulkier, for example, but the technique would be the same.

Putting the Pieces Together

The simplest way to hold marzipan pieces together is with egg whites, which act as an edible glue. Place some egg whites in a small clean dish and then place a small sponge in the center. The sponge will soak up the whites. To avoid getting the egg whites on your fingers, hold the marzipan in your hand and dab it on the sponge. When placing a very small piece, such as a nose or eyeball, apply the egg whites with a clean cotton swab.

When attaching one piece of marzipan to another, such as a limb to a torso or a nose to a head, make a small indentation in the piece that will be added to, so that the attached component is slightly inset. This will increase the stability.

Modeled figures frequently need more structural support to hold them together, especially when placing three or more pieces on top of each other.

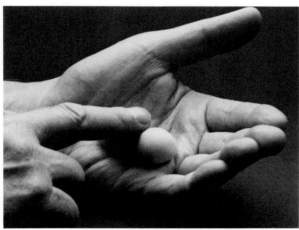

3-5

3-6

There are many gadgets available, but I suggest you use a toothpick. Insert the toothpick through the base to stabilize the figure until it dries, usually after a few hours. Remove it from the bottom. If you are entering a piece in a food show, be certain that any supports do not show, as you may lose some points when being judged. And certainly, if the piece is going to be eaten, remove the toothpick.

Some figures need to be supported by resting them against a small wooden block or a piece of foam rubber, or by curving them over a rolling pin or dowel until they dry. Flowers will keep their shape if they are placed in small plastic cups to keep them from bending over.

ANIMALS AND SMALL FIGURES

All the animals and small figures in this chapter are constructed from the basic shapes explained in Chapter 3. Each figure can be modeled easily and rapidly, following the step-by-step procedures outlined. After you have practiced forming these figures, I hope you will have gained enough expertise to try some of the more difficult techniques explained in later chapters.

All the marzipan for these figures was first tinted by kneading in a little food color, and many were sprayed with additional color for contrast and to bring out the highlights (see pages 10–11 for instructions on using a spray gun). The colors suggested are the ones I used to make the examples, but they are only suggestions. Vary them according to your needs. Remember to use some egg white as a glue when adding one piece to another.

The modeling tools that I refer to are the modeling sticks described on page 15. I use three basic sticks: a stick with a rounded bulb at each end for making cavities such as eye sockets and ear canals; a stick with a sharp point for making small holes such as nostrils; and a flat stick with a point for scoring lines to make toes and claws. Improvise or use a plastic spoon if you don't have the right modeling stick on hand.

I have given the total weight for each piece as well as the individual weights for each of the components. If you wish to change the size of a figure, adjust the amounts accordingly.

When making figures for production, I like to use soft royal icing for making the eyes, eyebrows, and other facial details (see page 108 for the recipe). This is because it is faster to pipe the icing directly onto the face than it is to form these features in marzipan and attach them individually.

However, if you are just making a few pieces, it may not be practical to make a batch of the icing, so certainly use the marzipan. If you use royal icing, pipe a small white ball into the eye socket for the eye and then, when it is dry, pipe on a small dab of chocolate-colored royal icing or melted chocolate to form the pupil. If using marzipan, form the eye out of a small ball of white marzipan and the pupil out of an even smaller chocolate-colored ball, flattened for the pupil. Remember to moisten the eye with egg white before placing it in the eye socket. Follow this same procedure when making other facial features.

You will note that a small adjustment in the placement of the head or legs can give a different look or expression to the same figure. No need to keep them all the same—be creative!

Rabbit I (Fig. 4-1 a-c)

Weight: 1⅞ ounces (52.5 grams); 3 pieces.
Color: White, light yellow, or brown for the body and head. Dark brown for the tail and nose.

1. For the body, make a sausage, taper the ends, and slightly flatten the bottom. With scissors or a knife, cut through the center of one end to separate the back legs. Roll the two back legs between your fingers to shape them and then fold the legs underneath the body. Make an indentation on the other end to define the front legs and bring them straight forward. With your finger, make a small indentation on the body for the head.
2. For the head and ears, make a pear shape and elongate the neck of the pear for the ears. Using a knife, make a cut to separate each ear and then roll them between two fingers to shape them. With a modeling tool, make a long cavity in each ear and then make two indentations in the face for the eyes. Place the head on the body.
3. For the tail, make a pear shape. Make a small indentation on the rabbit's rump and attach the tail.
4. To finish, make the eyeballs and nose out of soft royal icing or marzipan. Spray the rabbit with a slightly darker color for contrast. Note the two ways the head can be placed to give the figure more interest.

4-1a: Rabbit I

(L to R) Body: 1¼ oz. (35 g); face: ½ oz. (14 g); tail: ⅛ oz. (3.5 g)

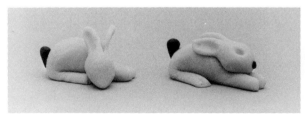

4-1b

4-1c

23

Rabbit II (Fig. 4-1 d-e)

Weight: 1¾ ounces (49 grams); 3 pieces.
Color: Same as for Rabbit I.

This is the same rabbit as Rabbit I except that the body is lying on its side. Make the body and cut through the center of both ends, instead of just one, to separate the front and back legs. Place it on the surface and twist toward the middle so that the cut side is resting on the table. Make indentations on each foot for the claws and cross one foot over the other before positioning the head.

4-1d: Rabbit II

4-1e

Rabbit III (Fig. 4-2 a-c)

Weight: 1¾ ounces (49 grams); 3 pieces.
Color: Same as for Rabbit I.

1. For the body, make a sausage with one end tapered (like a carrot). Cut through the center of the tapered end to separate the front legs. Roll the two pieces between your fingers to shape the legs. Place the broad end on the surface and bend the front legs over, flattening the feet slightly. Using a modeling tool, make indentations on the feet for the claws. Make a slight indentation on the body for the head. For support, bend the body over a wooden dowel or small rolling pin. Remove it in a few hours or when it is firm.

2. For the head and tail and how to finish, see steps 2, 3, and 4 in Rabbit I.

4-2a: Rabbit III

(L to R) Body: 1¼ oz. (35 g); face: ⅜ oz. (10.5 g); tail: ⅛ oz. (3.5 g)

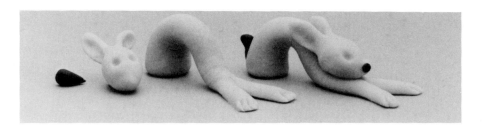

4-2b

4-2c

Rabbit IV (Fig. 4-3 a-c)

Weight: 1¾ ounces (49 grams); 3 pieces.
Color: Same as for Rabbit I.

1. For the body, make a pear.
2. With a modeling tool, make a line on each side of the broad end for the hip and a line on the narrow end for the front legs. With your finger, make a slight indentation for the head.
3. For the head and tail and how to finish, see steps 2, 3, and 4 in Rabbit I.

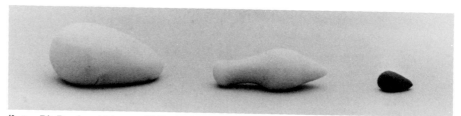

4-3a: Rabbit IV

(L to R) Body: 1 ¼ oz. (35 g); face: ⅜ oz. (10.5 g); tail: ⅛ oz. (3.5 g)

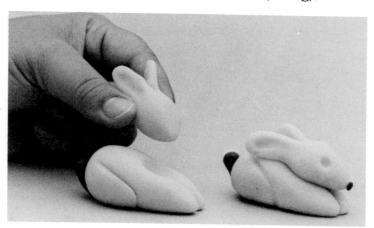

4-3b

4-3c

Rabbit V (Fig. 4-4 a-c)

Weight: 2 ounces (56 grams); 3 pieces.
Color: Same as for Rabbit I.

1. For the body, make a sausage shape and taper one end (like a carrot). On the tapered end, make a line through the middle with a modeling tool to show the front legs and a line on each side of the broad end to show the hips.
2. For the head, see step 2 in Rabbit I.
3. For the back legs, make a sausage and bend it into a horseshoe shape. Flatten it slightly and make an indentation in the center with your finger. Make lines on the feet for the claws. Place the body in the center. Rest the front legs on a small piece of foam rubber or a small rolling pin until they dry. Place the head on top of the body.
4. To finish, see step 4 in Rabbit I.

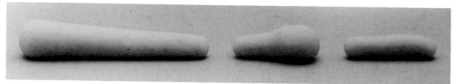

4-4a: Rabbit V

(L to R) Body: 1 ¼ oz. (35 g); face: ½ oz. (14 g); legs ¼ oz. (7 g)

4-4b

4-4c

Camel (Fig. 4-5 a-c)

Weight: 2¾ ounces (77 grams); 3 pieces.
Color: Pastel yellow for the body, neck, face, and ears. Red blanket. Dark brown for the nose.

1. For the body, make a pear shape and slightly elongate and flatten the narrow end. With a knife, cut through the center of the narrow end to separate the front legs. Roll them between two fingers to shape them.
2. For the head, make a sausage. Bend it two-thirds of the way up to form the neck and face. Make two small indentations for the ears and eyes. For the ears, make two little marzipan balls, make a cavity in the center, and place them on the head. Place the neck between the front legs and squeeze it slightly.
3. For the blanket, roll a piece of marzipan into a rectangle and press it with a ribbed rolling pin or make indentations with a tool for the tassels. Place it on top of the body.
4. To finish, make the eyes and nose out of soft royal icing or marzipan. Before placing the blanket, spray the body with a light brown color for contrast.

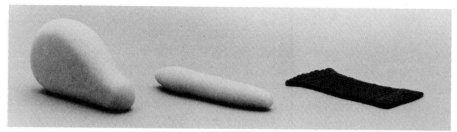

4-5a: Camel

(L to R) Body: 2 oz. (56 g); neck: ½ oz. (14 g); cover: ¼ oz. (7 g)

4-5b

4-5c

Duck I (Fig. 4-6 a-c)

Weight: 1⅞ ounces (52.5 grams); 3 pieces.
Color: Egg yolk yellow for the body and head. Red or orange for the beak.

1. For the body, roll a seamless ball into a pear shape, then make a curve and bend the narrow end up for the tail. Flatten the tail slightly and make lines with a modeling tool to show the feathers. Press an indentation for the head and beak.
2. For the head, make a ball and make two cavities for the eyes.
3. For the beak, make a pear and squeeze the narrow end slightly so the front is thicker. Make a line with a modeling tool to form the opening in the beak. Place the beak and then mount the head.
4. To finish, make the eyes out of soft royal icing or marzipan.

4-6a: Duck I

(L to R) Body: 1¼ oz. (35 g); face: ½ oz. (14 g); beak: ⅛ oz. (3.5 g)

4-6b

4-6c

Duck II (Fig. 4-7 a-c)

Weight: 2⅛ ounces (59.5 grams); 5 pieces.
Color: Egg yolk yellow for the body and head. Orange or red for the beak, legs, and feather.

1. For the body, make a pear and follow step 1 in Duck I to complete.
2. For the head and beak, follow steps 2 and 3 in Duck I.
3. For the feather on the head, make a small pear and flatten the narrow end. Place the feather on the head, bending it up.
4. For the legs, make a sausage and bend it into a horseshoe. Flatten it with your finger in the center and make lines with a modeling tool for the toes. Place the assembled body on top.
5. To finish, make the eyes out of soft royal icing or marzipan.

4-7a: Duck II

(L to R) Body: 1¼ oz. (35 g); face: ½ oz. (14 g); beak: ⅛ oz. (3.5 g); feather: 1/32 oz. (1g); legs: ¼ oz. (7g)

4-7b

4-7c

Capricorn (Fig. 4-8 a-c)

Weight: 2⅞ ounces (80.5 grams); 5 pieces.
Color: Light yellow or light coffee for the body and head. Fur should be the same color but darker. Chocolate brown for the tail and nose.

1. For the body, make a sausage and form it into a horseshoe. Make an indentation on one end for the head and on the other end for the tail. Place the body over a wooden dowel or rolling pin for support until it dries.
2. For the head, make a pear and cut through the broad end to form the horns. Twist and curl them back onto themselves. Make two cavities for the eyes.
3. For the fur, roll a piece of marzipan into a rectangle and press it with a ribbed roller or use a modeling tool to simulate the hair. Place it over the body. Place the head on the body.
4. For the tail, make a small sausage and attach it to the capricorn's rump.
5. For the nose, make a small ball and attach it to the face.
6. To finish, make the eyes out of royal icing or marzipan.

4-8a: Capricorn

(L to R) Body: 1¼ oz. (35 g); face: ½ oz. (14 g); hair: 1 oz. (28 g); tail & mouth: ⅛ oz. (3.5 g)

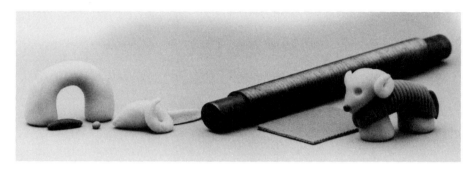

4-8b

4-8c

Pig and Wild Boar (Fig. 4-9 a-d)

Weight: 2 ounces (56 grams); 4 pieces.
Color: Light pink for the body, tail, and ears. Red tongue (optional).

1. For the body, make a ball and form it into a bulky triangle (a pig's body is very stout). Bend it slightly. With scissors, cut into the center and then cut each half again to form four legs. Roll each leg between two fingers to shape them. Make a line over each leg for the hips. Place the body on a small wooden dowel or rolling pin for support. Taper one end for the snout and cut open the mouth. Make two small cavities for the eyes (pigs have small eyes) and two nostrils.
2. For the ears, make two small pears and make a cavity in each. Attach them right above the eyes.
3. For the pig's tail, make a sausage and taper one end. Attach the narrow end to the rump and lay the tail over the back. For the boar's ridged back, make a sausage the length of the body and mark it with small indentations with a modeling tool. Attach it to the back.
4. For the tongue, make a small pear and flatten it. Insert it into the mouth.
5. To finish, make the eyes out of soft royal icing or marzipan.

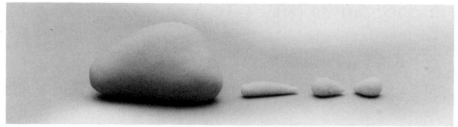

4-9a: Pig and Wild Boar

(L to R) Body: 1¾ oz. (49 g); tail & ears: ¼ oz. (7 g)

4-9b

4-9c

4-9d

37

Hippopotamus (Fig. 4-10 a-c)

Weight: 3 ounces (84 grams); 6 pieces.
Color: Pastel yellow-green for the body, head, ears, and mouth. White for the eye sockets.

1. For the body, make a bulky sausage and taper one end. Cut the tapered end in half to form the legs. Separate and flatten them slightly and make indentations for the toes. Poke holes all over to simulate the bumpy skin. Bend the front legs over the body and make lines on both sides of the broad end for the hips.
2. For the mouth, make a pear and flatten the narrow point. Cut the broad end to form the lips and open them.
3. For the head, make a ball and make two cavities for the eyes and small indentations for the ears. Poke three small holes on each side of the nose. Place the mouth between the front legs and place the head on top.
4. For the eye sockets, make two tiny balls and press a deep hole in the center. Insert them in the eye cavities.
5. For the ears, make two balls, press a cavity in the center, and attach them to the head.
6. To finish, make the eyes out of royal icing or marzipan. For additional effect, spray a light brown color over the back.

(L to R) Body: 1⅞ oz. (52.5 g); mouth ½ oz. (14 g); face: ½ oz. (14 g); ears & eyes: ⅛ oz. (3.5 g)

4-10a: Hippopotamus

4-10b

4-10c

Squirrel I (Fig. 4-11 a-c)

Weight: 2⅛ ounces (59.5 grams); 6 pieces.
Color: Light brown, mocha, or coffee brown for the body. A darker chocolate brown for the tail and ears.

1. For the body, make a pear. With a modeling tool, make a line on the narrow end for the front legs; do not separate them. Make an indentation over the legs for the head and on the rump for the tail.
2. For the tail, make a sausage and taper both ends. Make a line down the center and flatten the piece slightly. Draw lines from the center outward to simulate the bushy fur.
3. For the head, make a pear and and use a modeling tool to press indentations for the eyes and ears.
4. For the nose, make a small ball and attach it to the head. For the ears, make two slightly larger balls and press a cavity in the center. Attach them to the head also.
5. To finish, make the eyes out of royal icing or marzipan.

4-11a: Squirrel I

(L to R) Body: 1¼ oz. (35 g); tail: ½ oz. (14 g); face: ¼ oz. (7 g); nose & ears: ⅛ oz. (3.5 g)

4-11b

4-11c

41

Squirrel II (Fig. 4-12 a-c)

Weight: 2⅜ ounces (73.5 grams); 7 pieces.
Color: Same as for Squirrel I.

1. For the body, make a pear.
2. With a modeling tool make a line in the narrow end for the front legs and rest the body against a piece of foam rubber or a rolling pin for support.
3. For the tail, see step 2 in Squirrel I. Attach it to the back of the body.
4. For the legs, make a sausage and bend it into a horseshoe. Flatten the center and make lines with a modeling tool for the toes.
5. For the head, make a pear and press indentations for the eyes and ears.
6. For the nose, make a small ball and attach it to the head. For the ears, make two slightly larger balls and make a cavity in the center. Attach them to the head. Place the assembled head on the body.
7. To finish, make the eyes out of soft royal icing or marzipan.

4-12a: Squirrel II

(L to R) Body: 1¼ oz. (35 g); tail: ½ oz. (14 g); legs: ¼ oz. (7 g); face: ¼ oz. (7 g); nose & ears: ⅛ oz. (3.5 g)

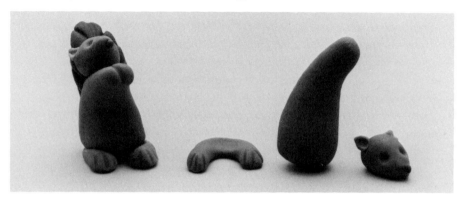

4-12b

4-12c

Elephant I (Fig. 4-13 a-c)

Weight: 3 ounces (84 grams); 9 pieces.
Color: White, light brown, or chocolate. For contrast, make the body and head light brown and the legs chocolate.

1. For the body, make a stubby pear and set it upright, broad side down. Using two fingers, press an indentation on the narrow end for the head, four indentations on the torso for the legs, and one for the tail.
2. For the head and trunk, make a curve, squeezing and rolling your palms around the narrow end to form the trunk. Poke two little holes at the end of the trunk for the nostrils. Make two cavities for the eye sockets and a slit for the mouth.
3. For the legs, make four sausages, slightly tapered on one end. Press little indentations on the broad side for the toes. Attach the legs to the body and gently squeeze them toward the center. Attach the head.
4. For the ears, make two balls. Place a ball in the palm of one hand and with the thumb of your other, press in the center to form the ear with an outer ridge. (You can also put the ball on a 2-inch-thick piece of foam rubber and press the center.) Bend the ear slightly and attach it to the assembled body.
5. For the tail, make a small sausage and taper one end. Attach it to the elephant's rump.
6. To finish, make the eyes and eyebrows out of soft royal icing or marzipan.

4-13a: Elephant I

(L to R) Body: 1 ½ oz. (42 g); face: ¾ oz. (21 g); front legs: ¼ oz. (7 g); back legs: ¼ oz. (7 g); ears & tail: ¼ oz. (7 g)

4-13b

4-13c

Elephant II (Fig. 4-14 a-c)

Weight: 2¼ ounces (63 grams); 5 pieces.
Color: Same as for Elephant I.

1. For the body, make a sausage and bend it into a horseshoe. Make a line on both ends to show the front and back legs. Press indentations for the tail and head. Curve the body over a wooden dowel or rolling pin for support.
2. For the head, see step 2 in Elephant I.
3. For the ears and tail, see steps 4 and 5 in Elephant I.

4-14a: Elephant II

(L to R) Body: 1½ oz. (42 g); face: ½ oz. (14 g); ears & tail: ¼ oz. (7 g)

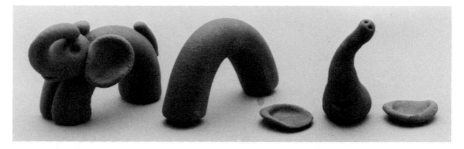

4-14b

4-14c

46

Fox (Fig. 4-15 a-c)

Weight: 2½ ounces (70 grams); 3 pieces.
Color: Light brown for the body. Darker brown for the head and tail.

1. For the head, make a pear and squeeze out the narrow end for the snout. Bend the snout up slightly and flatten it on both sides with your fingers. Squeeze out the ears and make two narrow cavities for the eye sockets (fox eyes look squinty).
2. For the tail, make a sausage and taper both ends, one end longer than the other. With a modeling tool, make lines for the bushy fur.
3. For the body, make a pear and make lines on the narrow end to show the front legs. Make an indentation for the head. Attach the head to the body and curl the tail along one side.
4. To finish, make the eyes out of soft royal icing or marzipan.

4-15a: Fox

(L to R) Face: ½ oz. (14 g); tail: ½ oz. (14 g); body: 1½ oz. (42 g)

4-15b

4-15c

Cat I (Fig. 4-16 a-c)

Weight: 1⅞ ounces (52.5 grams); 4 pieces.
Color: White or light brown.

1. For the body, make a pear and make a line on the narrow end with a modeling tool to show the front legs; do not separate them. Use a modeling tool to make little lines for the toes. Make an indentation over the legs for the head and on the rump for the tail.
2. For the tail, make a sausage and taper both ends. Flatten it slightly and attach the tail to form a graceful curve along the body.
3. For the head, make a ball and with two fingers squeeze out the ears. Make a cavity in each with a modeling tool. Using a modeling tool, cut a slit for the eye sockets and a little pocket for the mouth. Press a small indentation for the nose. Place the head on the body.
4. For the nose, make a tiny ball and attach it to the face.
5. To finish, make the eyes and eyebrows out of soft royal icing or marzipan. For contrast, spray the back a light brown.

4-16a: Cat I

(L to R) Body: 1 ¼ oz. (35 g); tail: ¼ oz. (7 g); face & nose: ⅜ oz. (10.5 g)

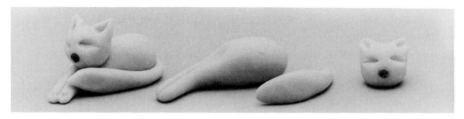

4-16b

4-16c

Cat II (Fig. 4-17 a-c)

Weight: 1⅞ ounces (52.5 grams); 4 pieces.
Color: White or light brown for the body. Darker brown for the tail.

1. For the body, make a sausage and slightly taper one end. Cut through the center of the narrow end for the front legs and separate them. Flatten the feet and make lines for the toes. Bend one paw over the other for a cute pose.
2. For the tail, make a sausage and taper both ends. Attach it to the body.
3. For the head, make a ball and squeeze out the ears with two fingers. Make a cavity in each with a modeling tool. Make a slit for the eye sockets and the mouth. Press a small indentation for the nose. Place the head on the body.
4. For the nose, make a tiny ball and attach it to the face.
5. To finish, make the eyes and eyebrows out of soft royal icing or marzipan.

4-17a: Cat II

(L to R) Body: 1¼ oz. (35 g); tail: ¼ oz (7 g); face & nose: ⅜ oz. (10.5 g)

4-17b

4-17c

Cat III (Fig. 4-18)

Weight: 2⅜ ounces (66.5 grams); 10 pieces.
Color: White or light brown for the body. Darker brown for the tail.

1. For the body, make a sausage and slightly taper both ends. Cut through the center of both ends for the front and back legs and separate them. Flatten the feet and make lines for the toes and hips. Bend the body over a wooden dowel or rolling pin for support.
2. For the tail, make a sausage and taper both ends. With a modeling tool make lines for the fur. Curve the tail and attach it to the body.
3. For the head, make a ball, and using a modeling tool, press indentations for the ears, cheeks, and nose, and mouth. For the ears, make two small balls and make a cavity in each. Attach them to the face. For the cheeks and nose, make three balls, flatten them, and attach them to the face. Place the head on the body.
4. For the mouth, make a red ball, press in a cavity, and attach it to the face.
5. To finish, make the eyes, eyebrows, and teeth out of soft royal icing or marzipan.

4-18: Cat III

Body: 1¼ oz. (35 g); face & nose: ⅜ oz. (10.5 g); tail: ¼ oz. (7 g); base: ½ oz. (14 g)

Bear I (Fig. 4-19 a-d)

Weight: 2⅞ ounces (80.5 grams); 8 pieces.
Color: For the bear, white or yellow for the body, head, ears, arms, and legs. Brown for the nose. For the panda bear, white or yellow for the body and face. Dark brown or chocolate for the arms, legs, nose, and tail.

1. For the body, make a sausage and slightly taper one end. Set it upright, broad side down. Using your finger, press an indentation on the narrow end for the head, four indentations on the torso for the legs, and one for the tail.
2. For the head, make a curve, tapering the narrow end to a point. Bend it up to form the nose. Use a modeling tool to make a hole for the mouth and cavities for the eye sockets and ears.
3. For the ears, make two small balls and make a cavity in the center, forming a thick ridge around the rim. Make a tiny marzipan ball for the nose. Attach the ears and nose to the head.
4. For the legs, make four sausages, tapering the ends for the feet. Bend the feet and flatten them between two fingers. Use a modeling tool to make the toes. Attach the legs to the body and then attach the head. When the legs are in place, place both hands on each side of the body and press in slightly so that all the legs are secured.
5. To make the panda's eyes, make a tiny ball of chocolate-colored marzipan. Make a cavity in the center and insert it into the eye socket.
6. To finish, make the eyes and eyebrows out of soft royal icing or marzipan. To get a fuzzy fur effect, brush egg whites over the whole bear with a soft brush and then roll the bear in fine, dry yellow, chocolate, or angel food cake crumbs.

4-19a: Bear I

(L to R) Body: 1¼ oz. (35 g); face: ½ oz. (14 g); legs 4 × ¼ oz. (28 g total); ears: 2 × ¹⁄₁₆ oz. (3.5 g total)

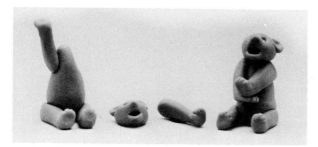

4-19b

4-19c

4-19d

Bear II (Fig. 4-20 a-c)

Weight: 3 ounces (84 grams); 9 pieces.
Color: White or light yellow

1. To make the body, head, legs, and ears, see steps 1 through 4 in Bear I. Rest the bear over a wooden dowel or rolling pin until it is dry.
2. To finish, spray the back with a light brown color to give it some contrast.

4-20a: Bear II

(L to R) Body: 1 ¼ oz. (35 g); face: ½ oz. (14 g); legs: 4 × ¼ oz. (28 g total); tail: ⅛ oz. (3.5 g); ears: 2 × 1/16 oz. (3.5 g total)

4-20b

4-20c

Polar Bear I (Fig. 4-21 a-c)

Weight: 2⅝ ounces (73.5 grams); 8 pieces.
Color: White body. Dark brown for the nose.

1. For the body, head, legs, and ears, see steps 1 through 4 in Bear I. This polar bear has a bigger belly, so make the body broader and the back more rounded.
2. For the nose, make a tiny ball and attach it to the face.
3. To finish, make the eyes out of soft royal icing or marzipan.

4-21a: Polar Bear I

(L to R) Body & face: 1½ oz. (42 g); legs: 4 × ¼ oz. (28 g total); ears & ⅛ oz. (3.5 g)

4-21b

4-21c

Polar Bear II (Fig. 4-22 a-c)

Weight: 2⅜ ounces (73.5 grams); 7 pieces.
Color: Same as for Polar Bear I.

1. For the body and head, make a sausage and taper one end. Bend the narrow end up to form the face. Press two indentations for the ears, two for the eyes, and one for the nose.
2. For the ears, make two tiny balls and make a cavity in both. Pinch one side to make a point and attach them to the head.
3. For the front legs, make a sausage and bend it into a horseshoe. Bend the ends up to make the feet. Use a modeling tool to make the toes. Cross the legs.
4. For the back legs, make a sausage and taper one end. Bend the narrow ends up to form the feet. Use a modeling tool to make the toes.
5. Place the body on top of the front legs and attach the back legs.
6. To finish, make the eyes out of soft royal icing or marzipan.

(L to R) Body & face: 1½ oz. (42 g); front leg: ½ oz. (14 g); back legs: 2 × ¼ oz. (14 g total); ears & nose: ⅛ oz. (3.5 g)

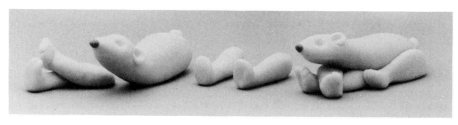

4-22b

4-22c

Dog I (Fig. 4-23 a-c)

Weight: 2⅛ ounces (59.5 grams); 5 pieces.
Color: White or light yellow for the body. Coffee or light brown for the nose.

1. For the body, make a sausage and taper one end. Cut a slice halfway through it for the tail and flatten it slightly with two fingers. Make lines on the tail with a modeling tool for the fur. Bend it up against the body. Make a line in the narrow end with a modeling tool to show the front legs.
2. For the head, make a stubby sausage. With your thumb and two fingers, press in one end to make the snout and mouth. Press two indentations for the ears. Use a modeling tool to make the whiskers and two cavities for the eye sockets.
3. For the ears, make two pears and flatten them on the table with your hand. Use a modeling tool to make lines for the fur.
4. For the nose, make a tiny ball and attach it to the face.
5. To finish, make the eyes out of soft royal icing or marzipan. Spray the body with a slightly darker color for contrast.

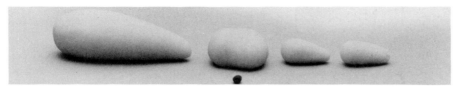

4-23a: Dog I

(L to R) Body: 1½ oz. (42 g); face & nose: ½ oz. (14 g); ears: ⅛ oz. (3.5 g)

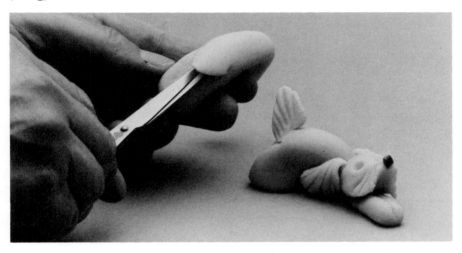

4-23b

4-23c

Dog II (Fig. 4-24 a-c)

Weight: 3⅜ ounces (94.5 grams); 7 pieces.
Color: White for the body and face. Light brown for the snout. Dark brown for the nose, ears, and tail.

This dog can be formed either on all fours or standing.

1. On all fours: For the body, make a sausage and taper one end. With a knife or scissors, cut the narrow end in half to form the front legs. Use a modeling tool to make the toes. Press indentations for the tail and the head. Bend the body over and flatten both ends against the table.
2. Standing: For the body, make a sausage and taper one end. Place the body upright, broad end down. Make an indentation on top for the head and for the feet and tail.
3. For the head, make a ball and make cavities for the eye sockets and indentations for the ears and snout.
4. For the snout, make a bean shape. Bend it forward slightly and poke holes with a modeling tool for the whiskers. Attach it to the head.
5. For the ears, make two pears and flatten them. Make a cavity in the broad part and attach them to the head. Bend them over so they look floppy. Attach the head to the body.
6. For the tail, make a sausage and taper one end. Attach it to the rump.
7. To finish, make the eyes and eyebrows out of soft royal icing or marzipan. Spray a light brown color over the back for contrast.

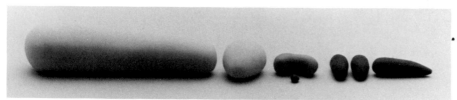

4-24a: Dog II

(L to R) Body: 2½ oz. (70 g); face, 3 pieces: ⅜ oz. (17.5 g);
ears: ⅛ oz. (3.5 g); tail: ⅛ oz. (3.5 g)

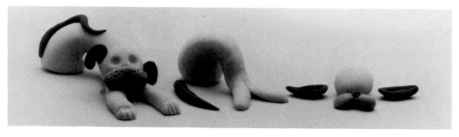

4-24b

4-24c

Dog III (Fig. 4-25 a-b)

Weight: 2 ounces (56 grams); 5 pieces.
Color: White or light yellow for the body. Brown for the nose.

1. For the body, make a sausage and taper one end slightly. With scissors, cut the narrow end in half to form the legs and use a modeling tool to show the toes. Bend the body over and squeeze gently at the top to form a neck.
2. For the head, make a pear with a blunt end. Make cavities for the eye sockets and the mouth and press indentations for the ears and nose.
3. To make the ears, make two pears and flatten them. Use a modeling tool to show the fur. Attach the ears to the head and attach the head to the body.
4. To finish, make the eyes out of soft royal icing or marzipan.

(L to R) Body: 1 ¼ oz. (35 g); ears: ¼ oz. (7 g); face: ½ oz. (14 g)

4-25b

Lion I (Fig. 4-26 a-c)

Weight: 3 ounces (84 grams); 9 pieces.
Color: Yellow for the body, legs, whiskers, and ears. Dark brown for the mane, tail, and nose. Red for the lips.

1. For the body, make a narrow pear and elongate and round the neck, which will be the lion's head. Using two fingers, press small indentations in the body for the back and front legs. Bend the head slightly forward.
2. For the front legs, make a sausage and bend it into a horseshoe. Use a modeling tool to mark the toes. Slightly flatten the legs in the center with your fingers and attach it to the front of the body.
3. For the back legs, make a longer sausage than for the front legs and taper both ends slightly. Use a modeling tool to make toes on each end. Flatten the center of the sausage with your fingers and place the body on the flattened center. Fold the back legs on each side of the body as in the picture and then gently squeeze the legs toward the body with both hands to secure them.
4. For the mane, make a sausage and taper both ends. Flatten it slightly and use a modeling tool to make lines for the fur. Fold the mane into a circle and wrap it around the head; the part where it is joined should go under the neck.
5. For the tail, make a sausage and taper one end. Use a modeling tool to make lines for a bushy look. Attach it to the rump and lay it along the back.
6. For the ears, make two small balls and with a tool make cavities. Attach them to the head.
7. For the nose, make a round ball and poke two holes in it for the nostrils.
8. For the snout, make a bean and flatten it. Poke holes for the whiskers. Press it against the face and attach the nose in the center.
9. To finish, make the eyes and eyebrows out of soft royal icing or marzipan. The figure may need to rest against a wooden dowel or rolling pin for support until it dries.

4-26a: Lion I

(L to R) Body and face: 1½ oz. (42 g); back legs: ½ oz. (14 g); front legs: ¼ oz. (7 g); hair/mane: ½ oz. (14 g); tail: ⅛ oz. (3.5 g); snout, ears, nose; ⅛ oz. (3.5 g)

4-26b

4-26c

Lion II (Fig. 4-27 a-c)

Weight: 3 ounces (84 grams); 9 pieces.
Color: Same as for Lion I.
This lion is formed as for Lion I except that it is lying down. Refer to the other
reclining figures for how to position it.

4-27a: Lion II

(L to R) Body and face: 1 ½ oz. (42 g); back legs: ½ oz. (14 g); front legs: ¼ oz. (7 g); hair/mane: ½ oz. (14 g); tail: ⅛ oz. (3.5 g); snout, ears, nose: ⅛ oz. (3.5 g)

4-27b

4-27c

Monkey I (Fig. 4-28 a-c)

Weight: 3½ ounces (98 grams); 9 pieces.
Color: Chocolate or dark brown for the body, legs, face, ears, and nose. Light orange for the snout and belly. Red for the mouth.

1. For the body, make a pear. Using your fingers, press an indentation for the stomach.
2. For the stomach, make a ball and flatten it into an oval. Place it on the stomach cavity. Roll the body gently in both hands until the stomach is smoothly attached. Using your fingers, press indentations for the arms and legs. With a modeling tool, make a small hole for the belly button.
3. For the legs, make a sausage and bend it into a horseshoe. Flatten the center with your finger and use a modeling tool to make the toes on both ends. Place the body in the indentation and fold the legs up and forward on either side. Bend the ends to form the feet and squeeze the figure gently.
4. For the arms, make a sausage and flatten the center. Cut a slit on top of the neck and insert the flattened center in it. Squeeze to close. Bring the arms under the legs so the monkey is sitting on them.
5. For the head, make a pear shape and press indentations for the snout and ears.
6. For the snout, make a pear and flatten the broad end. Press it against the face.
7. For the mouth and nose, make tiny balls and attach them to the snout.
8. For the ears, make pears, flatten them, and attach them to the head, bending them slightly.
9. To finish, make the eyes out of soft royal icing or marzipan.

4-28a: Monkey I

(L to R) Body: 1½ oz. (42 g); legs: ½ oz. (14 g); arms: ½ oz. (14 g); face: ½ oz. (14 g); ears: ¼ oz. (7 g); face, nose, mouth: ¼ oz. (7 g)

4-28b

4-28c

71

Hear No Evil, See No Evil, and Speak No Evil Monkeys (Fig. 4-29)

Weight: Each monkey weighs 14 ounces (392 grams). The hat and scarf each weigh 1½ ounces (42 grams).
Color: Same as for Monkey I. Hat and scarf are white.

These monkeys are large, about 7½ inches (19.5 cm) tall. They could be used as a centerpiece or as part of a display.

1. To form the monkeys, follow steps 1 through 9 in Monkey I. Note the difference in the position of the hands: the first monkey is covering its ears, the second is covering its eyes, and the third is covering its mouth.
2. For the hat, make a blunt sausage and flatten both ends. Mark the pleats and rim with a modeling tool. Squeeze it gently to give it shape and place it on the head.
3. For the scarf, cut a narrow strip and fold it around the neck. Make a small ball, press a cavity in the center, and attach it to the center of the scarf as if it were knotted.

4-29

Monkey II (Fig. 4-30 a-c)

Weight: 3¾ ounces (105 grams); 12 pieces.
Color: Chocolate or dark brown for the body, face, ears, arms, and nose.
Light orange for the snout, hands, feet, tail, and eye cavity.

1. For the body, make a sausage and taper one end. Make indentations for the head and feet. Stand the body upright, broad end down.
2. For the head, make a ball and press indentations for the eyes and snout.
3. For the snout, make a bean and attach it to the head.
4. For the ears, make two pears and flatten them on the palm of your hand with your thumb. Bend and attach them to the head.
5. For the eye cavities, make a bean and make two cavities for the sockets. Attach them to the head.
6. For the hands, form them as for the hand in the Baby Face Plaque (page 81).
7. For the feet, make two balls and flatten them into ovals. Use a modeling tool to make lines for the toes. Attach the feet to the body.
8. For the mouth, make a ball and flatten it into an oval. With a modeling tool, press an indentation for the lips and open them slightly. Attach them to the snout.
9. For the nose, make a small ball and poke two holes in it for the nostrils. Attach it to the face.
10. For the tail, make a sausage and attach it to the rump, curling it around the body.

4-30a: Monkey II

(L to R) Body: 2¼ oz. (63 g); face, 2 pieces: ½ & ¼ oz. (21 g); ears: ¼ oz. (7 g); tail: ⅛ oz. (3.5 g); hand: ⅛ oz. (3.5 g); legs: ⅛ oz. (3.5 g); eyes & nose: ⅛ oz. (3.5 g)

4-30b

4-30c

75

Charlie Chaplin "Limelight" (Fig. 4-31 a-c)

Weight: 4¼ ounces (119 grams); 20 pieces.
Color: Chocolate or dark brown for the arms, body, shoes, hat, cane, moustache, coat lapels, and bow tie. Flesh color for the face, ears, hands, and nose. White for the shirt. Yellow or light green for the base.

This is a fun, albeit complex, figure to make. Put it together step by step, allowing some time for the body to dry before you attach the shoes.

1. For the body, make a sausage approximately 5 inches (13 cm) long. Flatten it slightly. Cut a 2½-inch (6.5-cm) slit lengthwise to form the legs. Give each leg a quarter twist toward the center so that the cut side is lying flat on the surface. Bend each leg to form a loop.
2. For the shirt, roll out a white piece of marzipan into a sausage approximately 1¾ inches (4.5 cm) long, flatten it by hand, and attach it to the body.
3. For the coat lapels, make a thin sausage approximately 5 inches (12.5 cm) long. Place the sausage around the perimeter of the shirt.
4. For the bow tie, cut two small triangles and make a small ball for the center. Attach the bow tie under the neck.
5. For the arms, make two sausages approximately 2 inches (5 cm) long. Press a small cavity at the end of each for the hands.
6. For the hands, form them as for hand in the Baby Face Plaque (see page 81). Attach the hands to the arms.
7. For the face, make a ball and shape it into an egg. Flatten the top of the head for the hat. Make two balls for the ears and press a cavity in each. Place them on the head. Make a ball for the nose and attach it to the face. Make two cavities for the eyes. Make the moustache and eyebrows out of soft royal icing or marzipan. For the hat, make a ½-inch (1.2-cm) circle and flatten it on the bottom to form the rim. Place the hat on the head. Make the cane out of a 2½-inch (6.2-cm) long sausage.
8. For the base, roll out a piece of marzipan with a ribbed rolling pin and cut it with a round cutter.
9. Assemble the body and let it dry, flat on a surface, until the following day.
10. Just before you are ready to assemble the complete figure, make the shoes. Make two pears and flatten them with the palm of your hand. Attach each shoe to the foot, broad end toward the toes. Make sure that the bottoms of the shoes are flat. Since the shoes will still be soft it will be easy to adjust the figure's position on the base.

4-31a: Charlie Chaplin

(L to R) Base: ½ oz. (14 g); shoes & body: 2¼ oz. (63 g); arms & hands: ½ oz. (14 g); coat & shirt: ¼ oz. (7 g); face, ears, nose: ½ oz. (14 g); cane, tie, hat: ¼ oz. (7 g)

4-31b

4-31c

Baby Face Plaque (Fig. 4-32 a–d)

Weight: 5¾ ounces (161 grams); 10 pieces.
Color: Light green or yellow for the base. White for the pillow and sleeve. Flesh for the face, cheeks, nose, ears, and hand (mix yellow and red for light skin, or brown for dark skin). Yellow or brown for the curl. Red for the mouth. Yellow-green for the base.

These baby faces are easy to make and can be endlessly varied by adding a hat or scarf, or by changing the hair. Of course you are not limited to making just babies—the faces here range from infants to teenagers. These plaques make good cake decorations.

The Base
Roll out a piece of marzipan with a ribbed roller and cut it into a circle 4 inches (10 cm) in diameter.

The Face (Fig. 4-32 a-b)
1. For the pillow, make a ball and flatten it in the front so the baby's head can rest at an angle. Press an indentation for the head.
2. For the face, make a pear. Place the pear rounded side up on your work surface. Place your whole hand on the bottom part of the face, pushing it down to make indentations for the baby's cheeks. With a modeling tool, make two eye sockets, placed low. Remember that a baby has a big forehead and the eyes must be placed in the right position. The younger the face, the lower the eyes (look at your own face for comparison).

4-32a

79

4-32b

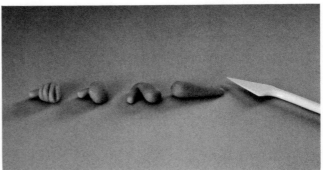

4-32c

3. For the cheeks, make a bean. Attach it to the face, gently pushing it down into position. (Don't blend the edges into the face; the cheeks should rest on the surface.) Brush the cheeks with a little red food color for a soft blush.

4. For the ears, make two pears and make a cavity in each with a modeling tool. Attach them to the face.

5. For the nose, make a ball and form the nostrils with a modeling tool.

6. For the mouth, make a ball and poke a hole in it with a modeling tool. Open it wide enough so the baby's thumb can be placed into the mouth. Attach the mouth to the face.

7. For the curl, make a pear and flatten it slightly. With a modeling tool, makes lines to show the hair. Attach it to the face.

8. To finish the face, coat it with cocoa butter (see page 11) for a shiny glow. Pipe soft white royal icing to make the eyeballs, and when the eyes are

dry, make the pupil out of brown. You can control the direction of the baby's glance by the way you position the pupil. Pipe in only enough icing so that the eye is resting inside the cavity—look in a mirror and notice how your eyeballs are not lying on top of your face, a mistake many students make when learning.

The Hand (Fig. 4-32c)

The technique for forming the baby's hand can be used for making a hand for any other figure.

1. For the sleeve, make a ball and press a deep cavity with a modeling tool for the hand to rest. You can make small indentations around the cuff for decoration (see Fig. 4–32b).
2. For the hand, make a pear, elongating the narrow end—this will form the thumb. Twist and fold it over, forming the rest of the fingers. Slightly flatten the broad side, and make three indentations around the hand to form the tops of the fingers (three indentations will make four fingers). Coat it with cocoa butter.
3. Place the hand into the sleeve's cavity and put it near the baby's mouth, putting the thumb to the lips.

4-32d

FLOWERS

Marzipan flowers can be placed on showpieces, centerpieces, cakes, or desserts. They are not only a demonstration of professional, practical talent, but are also an edible celebration for the event or occasion. When skillfully created, they are truly works of art.

When forming flowers as well as fruit or any other natural object, it is best if you have a real flower in front of you to copy. Flowers can be formed singly or grouped in bouquets, entwined with stems and leaves. The significant point to remember when forming bouquets is always to include an odd number of flowers—it gives more interest and makes the arrangement seem more natural and balanced.

Flowers can be made from tinted marzipan, or tinted and then sprayed for highlights. If you are making them in advance for production, as some commercial operations do on slower working days, make them out of uncolored marzipan and spray them as you need them with colors suitable for the occasion. Because marzipan will eventually dry out at room temperature if left uncovered, store the flowers in a cool, dust-free place, such as in a covered baking pan or plastic container placed in a cabinet or drawer. Spraying them with a light coating of cocoa butter will also help keep them moist. If stored properly, the flowers will remain fresh and edible for up to a week at least. I feel compelled to add, however, that a two-week old marzipan flower, even if dry, is a better decoration for a cake than a plastic ornament some bakeries choose to use. But that is my preference.

If you are decorating a cake, ice the cake completely and pipe the border before arranging the flowers. Lay the stems and flowers first, and then position the leaves. To give the arrangement more dimension, elevate a flower here and there so that they are all not lying flat. Make pedestals out of tiny balls of marzipan and place them under the flower. Also, when trimming the flower base, cut off the excess marzipan at an angle so the flower can be tilted in position.

The weight given for each flower is approximate and correlates with the examples shown in the pictures. You may need to make them larger or smaller, so adjust the amount of marzipan accordingly.

ROSE (Fig. 5-1 a-d)

A rose is a much-loved flower; it is personal, beautiful, and decorative. There are many different kinds; I like the full American Beauty. Although the rose is often the first flower students learn to make, it is perhaps the most difficult. However, once it has been mastered, you will be able to more easily grasp the techniques for making other flowers.

Over the years I have seen many different methods for making rose petals. Some people use a lightbulb to flatten each petal, others use a metal spatula or knife. I prefer to use a plastic scraper. Use whatever tool you are comfortable with—what matters is to make a rose that looks like a rose and not a cauliflower.

A rose is constructed out of 16 petals, arranged in three layers around a center cone made from 1 petal. The first layer contains 3 petals; the second

5-1a

5-1b

5-1c

5-1d

layer, 5 petals; and the third layer, 7 petals. This is considered to be a double rose. If you wish to make a smaller flower, or single rose, omit the third layer of petals.

Total weight: 2–2½ ounces (56–70 grams).

Color: Any pastel shade or uncolored.

1. Knead the marzipan until it is smooth and pliable on the work surface. Roll a seamless log about 1 inch (2.5 cm) thick and 7 to 8 inches (18 to 20 cm) long.

2. To make the first petal for the center cone, cut approximately 2 inches (5 cm) from the log, form it into a ball, and flatten it with your palm on the counter. Using a plastic scraper, push down on the marzipan, bending and moving the scraper back and forth in one direction at least 6 to 8 times, or until the marzipan is oval and paper thin around the edges and thick at the base. Carefully slide a thin, flexible metal spatula underneath the petal to release it from the work surface. With the thick side down, roll it into a pointed cone, leaving the outer edge slightly unfurled. This

will form the closed center bud. Press in the bottom to form a base—it should look like a pedestal.

3. To form the first layer of petals, cut three pieces from the log, each approximately ⅛ inch (3 mm) thick. Place them 3 to 4 inches (8 to 10 cm) apart on the table and flatten them with your palm. Push the plastic scraper back and forth over each petal until they are oval and paper thin around the edge and thick at the base. Remove the petals from the surface with the metal spatula. Gently pinch the base to form a curved cup. Using your thumb and finger, curve back the outer edge to form a natural bend on the tip (Fig. 5–1d).

4. To attach the petals, brush some egg white around the center cone. Attach the first petal to the cone, and then place the next one slightly underneath by lifting the previous one up with your fingers (Fig. 5–1b). Continue with the third petal, placing it slightly underneath the second. The point is to place the petals underneath each other, not on top.

5. To make the second layer, make five petals following the procedure in step 3, except make a deeper curve or lip on the outer edge by bending the top of the petal back more (Fig. 5–1d). Attach the petals to the base with egg white, each petal underneath the next (see step 4). This completes a single rose.

6. To make a double rose with a third layer of petals, make and attach seven more petals, following the same procedure as described above. However, instead of making a curved lip, place two fingers on top of each petal, and squeeze gently to form a V-shape on the outer edge. Attach them with egg white.

7. When all the petals are in place, hold the rose upside down and gently squeeze the base while rotating the flower. This will open the petals. Remove any excess marzipan from the base with a knife. Turn the rose right side up, and open the petals a little more with a plastic spoon if desired.

"Mother" Rose Bouquet (Fig. 5-2)

This beautiful display is a bouquet of roses suitable for decorating the top of a cake. It contains three double roses (three layers), two single roses (two layers), and one rosebud. For display purposes, I placed the bouquet on a 14-inch (35-cm) round wooden plaque covered with plastic chocolate, but it could also be covered with marzipan, pastillage, or royal icing tinted a chocolate color.

If you wish to include writing on the cake, as I did for this example, pipe the outline of each letter with royal icing as explained on page 21.

5-2

Two-Tone Rose (Fig. 5-3 a-b)

A two-tone rose can be made with any two colors, although a pastel shade and untinted (off-white) marzipan look best. For this example I colored part of the marzipan pink. When dividing the marzipan to tint it, leave one-third of it natural and color the rest.

This method of making two-tone marzipan is also used to create a two-tone Casey flower (page 90) and carnation (page 93).

Total weight: 8–9 ounces (224–252 grams) (makes 3 or 4 roses).
Color: 20 ounces (560 grams) tinted pink, 10 ounces (280 grams) untinted.

1. Using a rolling pin, roll out the pink marzipan into a smooth rectangle approximately ½ inch (1.2 cm) thick. Use a little powdered sugar to keep it from sticking to the surface.
2. Roll out the untinted marzipan to the same dimensions as the pink. It should be approximately ⅛ inch (3 mm) thick.
3. Brush the surface of the pink marzipan with a little egg white or water. Place the untinted sheet on top. Roll the layers together, pressing down gently, until they are about ⅛ inch (3 mm) thick—about the thickness of a silver dollar. Cut out the petals with a plain round cutter, 1 inch or 1¼ inches (2.5 or 3 cm) in diameter (Fig. 5-3a). Push a plastic scraper forward over each petal, squeezing the untinted marzipan toward the front so that it forms the outer edge. Form and attach the petals following the procedure as described for a rose (pages 85–86).

Note: Another way to make a two-color flower is to lightly knead, but not completely blend, two different colors together to create a marbleized effect. Although not as elegant as the technique just described, this method is a quick way to lighten the color of a flower.

5-3a

5-3b

NARCISSUS (Fig. 5-4a)

This simple, beautiful white flower is made using two pieces of marzipan, the center tinted yellow. After some practice, this is an easy and fun flower to make.
Weight: ⅞ ounce (24.5 grams).
Color: ¾ ounce (21 grams) tinted white, ⅛ ounce (3.5 grams) tinted yellow.

1. To form the base, make a seamless ball ¾ inch (2 cm) in diameter. Roll it into a cone shape, broad at the base and narrow at the top. Place the cone in your hand, broad end up. Insert a pointed modeling tool almost to the bottom and make a hole. Using your finger and thumb, open the hole gradually to form a cup.

2. With scissors, make six cuts in the cup to form the petals. One at a time, press your thumb in the center and put your finger underneath each petal, pushing toward the center to thin the top and slightly bend it. Gently pinch the top of each petal to form a point. Make small indentations on each petal with a plastic spoon or modeling tool.

3. To make the center bud, roll the yellow marzipan into a thin rectangular strip. Press small indentations down the length of one edge with a plastic spoon or modeling tool. Roll the strip around the tip of your finger and push your finger down on the table to seal the bottom, making a small, hollow cup. Place the cup in the center of the six petals, using some egg white as glue. Paint the top edge of the yellow cup with red food color.

Bouquet of Narcissi (Fig. 5-4b)

This bouquet of five narcissi resting on a plastic chocolate-covered plaque is an example of depth and harmony. The narrow long stems with the long skinny leaves are tinted a delicate pale green. The bouquet looks particularly attractive when placed on a cake with a pastel cream or light yellow icing.

5-4a

5-4b

"Casey" Flower (Fig. 5-5 a-c)

This fantasy flower is very appealing and quick to make. Once you have mastered it, you can make one approximately every minute, thus making it an excellent flower for mass production, although I suggest that you make only as many as you will use within a week. Stored longer, the marzipan will begin to dry out. If you are going to make the flowers in advance, keep the marzipan untinted so that you can spray them with whatever color you need. Place the flowers in a covered container or sheet tray and store them in a cool, dust-free place, such as in a drawer or cabinet.

Weight: ½–¾ ounce (14–21 grams).

Color: Tint it any pastel color, or make a two-tone version as described on page 87. You can also leave it untinted and spray it later before using.

1. Roll out the marzipan ⅛ inch (3 mm) thick using a rolling pin and a little powdered sugar. Cut it with a round or scalloped cutter 2 to 2¼ inches (5 to 5.75 cm) in diameter.

2. Flatten the outside edge of the circle with your palm and then smooth it with a plastic spoon. Holding the spoon at a 45-degree angle, place your thumb in the spoon's bowl (Fig. 5-5a) and make indentations from the center to the outer edge, rotating the marzipan a quarter turn until the circle is complete. As you push the spoon outward, the circle should enlarge about ⅛ inch to ¼ inch (3 to 6 mm). The outer edge should be paper thin with a ragged edge—somewhat like a carnation.

5-5a

5-5b

3. Remove the marzipan from the surface by sliding a small spatula underneath, loosening it gradually.

4. Place the flower on the top of a plastic cup, which should be about 2 inches (5 cm) smaller in diameter than the flower (Fig. 5-5 b, c). Using your two middle fingers, push the outer edge upward and the center down to form a ruffle. Do this in four places. Place two fingers between each ruffle and push the outer edge up and over the cup rim. Let the flower rest in the cup for 24 hours, or until the marzipan is dry enough to hold its shape.

5-5c

5. There are many different ways to finish the flower. If the flower is un-tinted, you can spray it any color you wish, although soft pastels look best. If the flower is already tinted, you can spray it with a slightly darker color to give it more contrast. You can also place a small ball or cone of marzipan in the center, attaching it with some egg white. The center can be rolled in egg white and dipped in coarse granulated sugar and sprayed with a color when it is dry. In the picture I made a chocolate-colored cone and piped on dots made from soft royal icing.

DAISY (Fig. 5-6)

Although a real daisy contains more than eight petals, for decorating purposes an eight-petal daisy looks attractive. The base of the daisy is made almost like the base of the narcissus. The weights below are for a finished daisy; you will need about an ounce (28 grams) of marzipan to start with.
Weight: ⅝ ounce (17.5 grams).
Color: ½ ounce (14 grams) tinted pastel yellow for petals, ⅛ ounce (3.5 grams) tinted chocolate for center.

1. Make a seamless ball 1½ inches (4 cm) in diameter. Form it into a cone by rolling it between your hands. Using your thumb and finger, square off the cone to make four equal sides.

5-6

2. With a sharp knife or scissors, cut the cone in half part of the way down to the base. Smooth the cut surfaces with your thumb and finger, and cut each half again to make four petals. Smooth the new cut surfaces. Cut each petal in half again to make eight petals and smooth the surfaces. Push the base of each petal toward the center, thinning the outer tip and thickening the center for support. Form a point at each petal tip. Make a long indentation in each petal from the bottom to the top with a toothpick or modeling tool.

3. To make the center, roll a small ball of chocolate-colored marzipan, flatten it slightly, and place it in the center of the daisy with a little egg white. Poke small holes in it with a pointed modeling tool. Cut away the excess marzipan from the bottom. To support the petals, put the daisy in a plastic cup for 24 hours or until it is dry enough to hold its shape.

Happy Birthday Daisy Bouquet (Fig. 5-7)

This bouquet is quite simple to make. The flowers rest on three stems and have seven leaves. These flowers are tinted a light orange with a chocolate-colored center, although any pastel color combination would work well also. For display, the bouquet is resting on a plaque covered with plastic chocolate (see pages 105–107).

CARNATION (Fig. 5-8)

A carnation, like a rose, can evoke many beautiful memories. There are many techniques for making carnations, but I have found that the following method works best. Once you get the hang of it, you will find it a very easy flower

5-7

5-8

to make. Note that the weight given is for a finished carnation; you will start with more marzipan and cut off the base when finished.

Weight: ¾–1 ounce (21–28 grams) per flower.

Color: Tint it any pastel color, or make a two-tone version as described in the following instructions.

1. Roll the marzipan into a rectangle approximately 8 by 24 inches (20 cm by 60 cm) and ¹⁄₁₆ inch (2 mm) thick, using a little powdered sugar to keep it from sticking.
2. Cut the marzipan into a lengthwise strip approximately 1½ inches (4 cm) wide (the longer the strip, the larger the flower). With your palm, smooth out one long edge to thin it.
3. Make small indentations or ridges along the thin edge using a plastic spoon. The edge should be paper thin and look somewhat ragged. With a

small knife, make tiny incisions about ⅛ inch (3 mm) deep and ½ inch (1.2 cm) apart down the length of the strip.

4. Loosen the strip from the surface by sliding a small metal spatula underneath it in several places until the marzipan is released. Hold the strip in one hand, and with the other, fold it onto itself in a zigzag manner, at the same time rolling it to form the flower. Hold the carnation upside down, and turn and squeeze it with your fingers about three-quarters of the way down. The carnation will start to open. Turn it right-side up and cut off any excess from the base. Continue making carnations with the rest of the marzipan.

5. To get that freckled appearance of typical carnations, spray the flower with a spray gun, atomizer, or air brush filled with a color slightly darker than the tinted marzipan. For a spottier effect, dip a toothbrush in diluted food color and rub it over a wire screen (see page 16).

Bouquet of Carnations (Fig. 5-9)

This bouquet of five carnations illustrates how to cluster a group of flowers. Elevate a flower here and there by placing small balls of marzipan underneath.

Two-Tone Carnation

Follow the same procedure for making a two-tone rose (page 87). The only difference is to roll the double layer of marzipan thinner and longer. To form the carnation, follow the steps outlined above.

5-9

FANTASY FLOWER (Fig. 5-10 a, b)

If you really want to make an easy flower, this is it. By substituting a fluted or scalloped cutter, you can vary the look and form some very interesting and attractive shapes. And if you are willing to spend a little extra time and effort putting on the finishing touches, your flowers will look quite special.

Depending on the size of the cutter, you can make flowers from ¼ inch to 3 inches (6 mm to 8 cm) in diameter. The technique is the same, regardless of the size.

Weight: Approximately ¼ ounce (7 grams), depending on the size of the cutter.
Color: Any pastel color.

5-10a

5-10b

1. Roll out the marzipan using a little powdered sugar. Larger flowers should be slightly thicker than smaller ones. Cut the marzipan with a cutter. The flower in the photograph is approximately 1½ inches (4 cm) wide. I used a scalloped cutter, and the marzipan, tinted light yellow, was rolled 1/16 inch (2 mm) thick.

2. Using a modeling stick, make indentations on the outer edge of each curve. Place the flower on a 1-inch (2.5-cm) thick piece of foam rubber and push the center in with a bulb-shaped modeling tool. As you push down, the outer edge will start to curl up.

3. Remove the flower for finishing. Spray the flower with a contrasting color (I used a light yellow base with a mist of soft orange). In the center attach a plain round ball of chocolate-colored marzipan with a little egg white. Use your imagination and come up with other creative ideas.

Fantasy Flower Bouquet (Fig. 5-11)

This bouquet of seven flowers shows good balance. Always use an uneven number of flowers when making a bouquet for the most natural looking arrangement.

FLOWER LEAVES AND STEMS

Making beautiful flowers is not enough. You must be able to make properly scaled stems and leaves to complete the picture. Placing a tiny delicate flower on a thick stem with a large leaf makes no sense, no more so than does combining a large flower with a thin, elegant stem and small leaves. The best way to decide what is correct is to copy what is real in nature and to respect laws of proportion for those flowers that are creations of your own fantasy.

My instructions for making stems and leaves are very simple, because I believe it is more important that the balance and proportion of the whole

5-11

flower and bouquet be in harmony than to insist on strict botanical accuracy. What people notice is whether the whole display is attractive, not whether a particular leaf really goes with the flower. These are small details, and I don't worry about them. What I am concerned about, and what you should be too, is the complete picture—that it be balanced, correctly scaled, and elegant.

1. To make stems, make a ball of pastel green-tinted marzipan and roll it into a rope using both hands. Avoid using powdered sugar if possible, because it will dull the surface gloss. A flower stem is usually wider and thicker on the bottom, and thinner and smaller on top. Cut the bottom of the stem off at an angle with a sharp knife. Sometimes I like to twist the end part of the stem a few times to form a tendril. It gives the display a lift, making it look crisp and natural (see Fig. 5-11). If five or more more stems are needed for your display, don't be afraid to place some on top of each other, as long as the total piece looks attractive and well balanced.

2. To make leaves, roll out a sheet of pastel green-tinted marzipan. The leaves used for small flowers are thinner than leaves used for large flowers. Cut the leaves out with a small sharp knife. With your hand, push the leaf flat to the surface and at the same time round the cut edges to give it a more natural shape. Place your thumb in the bowl of a plastic spoon, hold the spoon at an angle, and push from the center of the leaf to the outer edge (Fig. 5-12). By doing so the leaves will become slightly larger and paper-thin at the edge. Loosen the leaf by sliding a small metal spatula underneath the leaf and place it on your display, curling the edge and bending it up here and there. I like to see a floral decoration loose and elevated, not flat and stiff. Keep your bouquets looking airy and relaxed.

5-12

FRUIT

Making an assortment of marzipan fruit is a fun project, as long as the assortment is balanced and interesting. Your choice is inexhaustible, which is why it is sometimes difficult to make your selection. Marzipan fruit can be arranged in a cornucopia for a centerpiece, or grouped in a basket for display (Fig. 6-1). They are often made as a treat to be eaten at holidays, particularly at Christmas.

FORMING THE FRUIT

Each piece of marzipan fruit begins as a smooth and seamless ball formed with the palms of both hands. Roll and shape it with your fingers, pressing and turning the mass until it is formed. The best way to learn to form the fruit is to copy it from a piece in front of you. After the shape has been formed, use modeling tools, a toothpick, or a plastic spoon to make the necessary notches or indentations.

After the fruit has been formed, lay it on a tray covered with cotton batting 3 or 4 inches thick or with any other soft material. This will prevent the fruit from flattening or losing its shape. Leave smaller fruit to dry for 1 to 2 days and the larger fruit for 2 to 3 days, or until the marzipan has a thin crust. Only then can you begin to paint the fruit.

6-1

SPECIAL TOOLS

There are a few handy tools to use besides the normal modeling sticks (see Fig. 6-2). To replicate the indentations found in oranges and strawberries, cover two 4-inch (10-cm) squares of ¼-inch (6-mm) plywood with glue and attach small beads or seeds (such as sesame) all over the surface. Hold a piece of plywood in each hand and roll and press the marzipan until it is covered with small bumps. Another way to impress a pattern on the surface is to gently roll a piece of marzipan between two graters.

Painting the Fruit

Fruit painting is an art form (see Fig. C1 in color insert). You must understand colors and have patience with every piece during the painting process.

The paint, of course, is liquid, paste, or powder food colors. Most marzipan fruit is first colored with a yellow base, as yellow is the color of most fruits before they ripen. You can make the yellow look more natural by adding a drop of green or brown color.

It is difficult to exactly specify what colors to use, especially for apples and pears, which come in so many varieties, shapes, and colors. I recommend that you buy the real fruit as a model and try to duplicate it. Put a few drops of color on a plate, mix it with alcohol (whiskey, gin, or vodka, or any strong blend—it needn't be expensive as long as it is not for consumption—do not use rubbing alchohol), and stir it with a small brush. As I discussed in Chapter 2, I prefer to use alcohol rather than water when mixing colors because it will dry at once after it has been brushed on the fruit.

Just moisten your brush with the color—never dip it deeply into the dish. The point is to rub the color on, not saturate it. Remove any excess by rubbing the brush on a piece of white paper. Only then can you use it to rub the color onto the fruit. As long as the previous color application is dry, you can repeat rubbing some spots with different colors. A pear can have three or four layers of color—green, red, and brown spots over a base of yelllow. An apple can be highlighted with contrasting shades as well. But be careful. If the third application is too moist, for example, you will remove a layer of color when you rub on the fourth. Just remember to add each color after the previous one has completely dried. It is a good idea, by the way, to wear plastic or rubber

6-2

gloves when holding the fruit, especially during the first and second color applications, so that you don't stain your hands and nails.

To avoid getting any fingerprints on the fruit when applying the final color layers, put the fruit on a 6-inch (15-cm) skewer. Always insert the skewer into the thickest end of the fruit. Brush on some lines or darker shades here and there to simulate the stalk or stem end. Remove the skewer after the food color has dried.

It is the little splotchy spots on the fruit that give it a natural appearance. To do this, I like to rub a toothbrush dipped in greenish-brown food color over a small metal screen. This creates an excellent spotty effect. Try it first on white paper to remove excess color from the brush.

When the fruit is completely dry, spray or brush on a thin coat of cocoa butter (see page 11 for instructions). This will give it a natural shine as well as protect it.

Let us go over the colors I prefer to use for the most common fruits (Figs. C2 and C3). The shapes are very simple and are best formed by copying them from an example of the real thing. I have made suggestions when a special technique will help.

Apple The base color is lemon yellow. The second color is a light pastel green, brushed on through a metal screen with a toothbrush. Finishing touches are green and brown. The red cheeks are made by brushing on fine red lines applied with an almost-dry brush. With a fine paintbrush, make small lines on the top of the fruit around the stem end.

Orange Make the indentations on the skin by rolling the formed marzipan between two pieces of plywood covered with beads (see page 100) or by pressing the orange between two graters. The base color is orange, the second layer is some green spots, and the third layer is another application of orange. Brush on some brown spots here and there.

Peach The base color is lemon yellow, and the second layer is yellow mixed with a little brown. Dry it completely before you spray two red cheeks on each side to give it a peachy blush. To get a fuzzy finish, coat the peach with cocoa butter, sift on powdered sugar, and remove any excess by blowing it off with an empty spray gun or by brushing the surface with a dry feathery brush.

Plum   The base color is purple, and the second and third layers are purple mixed with a little blue.

Pear   The base color is lemon yellow, and the second layer is yellow mixed with green. Finish it with either some red or brown color brushed on with a toothbrush through a screen.

Strawberry   Press the strawberry against two graters (page 16) or between two pieces of plywood (see page 100) to make the pitted surface. The base color is lemon yellow, the second layer is orange, and the third layer is red.

Banana   Shape the marzipan into a ball and then a sausage. Taper one end—the stem end is thicker than the bottom end. With both hands, slide your fingers back and forth lengthwise, flattening the surface on each side—a banana is not really round. Squeeze out the stem.

A banana has several colors. The base is lemon yellow and the second layer has some green at the point followed by a slightly darker yellow. Brush on some brown to show the ripe spots on the skin and lines on the edges.

Purple Grapes   Before you color the grapes, make a small loop out of a 6-inch (15-cm) strand of wire and insert the wire through the center of each grape. The base color is blue and the second layer is purple, blue, and red. Sometimes you have to repeat another layer. After the grapes have completely dried, coat them with cocoa butter and lightly dust them with sifted powdered sugar. Cluster the grapes into a bunch and tie the ends of the wire together.

DECORATIVE COMPONENTS FOR DISPLAYS

Pastry and artistic food displays give all culinary craftsmen, be they students, apprentices, or professionals, a chance to be creative and show their artistic talents. The displays can range from a simple marzipan-decorated cake to elaborate showpieces three feet long. Any legitimate food material can be used as a component in a centerpiece, but the three I prefer to use are plastic chocolate, pastillage, and royal icing. Fondant is another decorative material, and it will be discussed in the next chapter as it is used specifically for cakes. Virtually all the examples in the next two chapters were made using these components, so once you know how to make them you will be limited only by your imagination.

PLASTIC OR MODELING CHOCOLATE

Plastic or modeling chocolate is a pliable edible material used to cover cakes, to mold and form into objects as you would marzipan, and to cover constructions, often made from pastillage. It is a versatile substance and can be made from dark, milk, or white chocolate, which can be tinted or left plain.

Plastic chocolate must be made from real chocolate—that is, chocolate that contains a high percentage (at least 31 percent) of cocoa butter and *only* cocoa butter as a fat, and chocolate liquor, not cocoa or chocolate flavoring. The amount of cocoa butter is quite important, because it is what gives the plastic chocolate its pliability, sturdiness, and shine. In Europe the highest quality chocolate is called *couverture*, although in the United States there are no parallel standards denoting chocolate of this grade. In fact, so-called couverture produced domestically is really compound chocolate or chocolate coating, which isn't genuine chocolate at all as it contains little or no cocoa butter and is made with other vegetable shortenings (such as palm oil or coconut oil), dry milk solids, cocoa flavoring, and food coloring. Avoid this stuff completely. If you cannot find genuine couverture chocolate, use the finest real chocolate you can buy, preferably imported.

DARK PLASTIC OR MODELING CHOCOLATE

16 ounces (448 grams) bittersweet or semisweet chocolate
8 ounces (224 grams) corn syrup

1. Melt the chocolate on top of a double boiler over low heat, stirring constantly, until the chocolate is barely melted (110°F). Be careful not to let the chocolate overheat or let it come in contact with water, including the steam from the double boiler—this will cause it to stiffen, or seize.
2. Warm the corn syrup until it reaches about the same temperature as the chocolate (110°F). Mix it thoroughly with the melted chocolate.
3. Pour the chocolate mixture on a marble slab or stainless steel surface and let it cool until it reaches room temperature.
4. Place the chocolate mixture in an airtight container for at least 24 hours.
5. The next day, roll the chocolate through a clean dough sheeter or pasta roller several times until it is pliable and shiny. If you don't have a sheeter, you can knead it by hand, which will take a lot of work. Work small pieces at a time. The warmth of your hand will melt the cocoa butter in the chocolate and make it more flexible and malleable.
6. Use what you need and store any excess at room temperature, tightly wrapped in plastic and placed in a covered container so that it doesn't dry out.

PLASTIC MILK CHOCOLATE

Substitute milk chocolate for the bittersweet or semisweet chocolate.

WHITE PLASTIC CHOCOLATE

35 ounces (1 kilogram) white chocolate
21 ounces (588 grams) corn syrup
2½ ounces (70 grams) cornstarch
3½ ounces (98 grams) marzipan

1. Melt the white chocolate in the top of a double boiler over low heat, stirring constantly, until it is melted (110°F).
2. Heat the corn syrup until it reaches the same temperature as the white chocolate (110°F) and mix it thoroughly with the melted chocolate.
3. Pour the chocolate mixture on a marble or stainless steel surface and let it stand until it reaches room temperature. Knead in the cornstarch and marzipan, and roll and fold it through a clean dough sheeter or pasta roller until it is pliable and shiny. Or knead it by hand, working it in small pieces until it is thoroughly mixed and supple.
4. Store as for dark plastic chocolate.

PASTILLAGE

Pastillage is another extremely versatile component for making displays. It is often used as a base or support because it dries so rigidly. It can be covered with plastic chocolate or marzipan. It is used to model plates and candy dishes, and anything else that must hold its shape. It is also a good surface for painting and decorating, and you can make unusual effects that will set your work apart from others (see page 130, crackling). Pastillage is also used for decorative work, including traditional wedding cake ornaments and other fine handwork. It can be tinted with food color, but is usually left white.

There are various recipes for pastillage—hard-drying and soft-drying—and some that contain cornstarch, which I avoid on principle since I dislike adding an uncooked ingredient to an edible product, albeit one that few people would care to eat. The following formula is for a hard-drying paste and I have been very successful with it. The gelatin gives it flexibility and the corn syrup some moisture.

HARD-DRYING PASTILLAGE

¾ ounce (21 grams) gelatin
1 ounce (28 grams) granulated sugar
8 ounces (224 grams) boiling water (212° F)
3 ounces (84 grams) corn syrup
4½ to 5 pounds (2016 to 2240 grams) powdered sugar
⅛ ounce (3.5 grams) cream of tartar

---

1. In a small clean bowl, combine the gelatin and granulated sugar, mixing thoroughly. Add the boiling water, mixing until the gelatin is completely

dissolved. The sugar will distribute the gelatin evenly in the water so that lumps do not form.

2. In a stainless steel mixing bowl fitted with a paddle, place the powdered sugar and cream of tartar, mixing until combined. Slowly add the warm gelatin solution, mixing thoroughly and scraping the paddle and sides of the bowl a few times. If it seems too stiff, add a little corn syrup; if too soft, add more powdered sugar. The texture of the pastillage mixture will depend on your application. For creating pieces where you will need to roll out large sheets, make the pastillage stiffer. If you need a more pliable consistency so that you can mold or bend it, make it softer.

3. Store the pastillage in a double-sealed plastic bag at room temperature. It will start to form a crust within 10 minutes if left uncovered. The pastillage will be easier to work with if you let it rest for 24 hours before using.

4. When you are ready to use the pastillage, work it on a table until it is pliable. Because air is beaten into the pastillage while it is being mixed, there will often be bubbles in the surface when you roll it out. These must be popped immediately (use a toothpick or a pin) before the surface dries.

ROYAL ICING

Royal icing has many uses: piped out as a decoration, molded into flowers or figures, and even used as a glue to hold two pieces of pastillage together. Since it is so easy to make and dries so hard, I have sometimes used it instead of fondant to cover display cakes. This recipe is very simple and can be adjusted according to the application.

2½ ounces (70 grams) egg whites (approximately 3 eggs)
14 ounces (392 grams) powdered sugar
⅛ ounce (3.5 grams) cream of tartar

---

1. Combine the egg whites, sugar, and cream of tartar in a small, clean stainless steel mixing bowl. Whip on high speed until the icing is creamy and thick. Add more powdered sugar to stiffen, more egg white to soften.

2. Use immediately, keeping the bowl covered with a clean wet towel to prevent the icing from drying.

When piping royal icing, make a paper cone out of white paper, clipping off the point to form the tip. You can adjust the consistency of the royal icing by adding more egg whites to soften it or powdered sugar to stiffen it. For piping out decorations or fine lines, the consistency should be about the stiffness of a buttercream. For covering larger areas such as a cake, for filling in the spaces of a piped out decoration, or for spreading the royal icing when using it as a glue, add more egg white to make the consistency softer, about the viscosity of thick buttermilk.

DECORATED CAKES AND MARZIPAN COOKIES

Using marzipan, pastillage, plastic chocolate, and royal icing for decorating cakes and cookies is a wonderful way to express your creativity by making edible art. By combining any or all of them, you will be able to diversify and expand your repertoire. The cakes and cookies described in this chapter are meant to give you ideas for developing your own creations. Read the next chapter for additional ones. The results of your efforts will be quite impressive.

PREPARING THE CAKES FOR DECORATION

Working with Fondant

Before the cakes are decorated, they are spread with buttercream, covered with a thin sheet of marzipan, and then iced with fondant. (I use commercially prepared fondant, as do many professionals, because of the time and labor involved in making it from scratch. It can be purchased through any baking supply source. If you wish to make it yourself, follow a recipe in any good pastry cookbook.) The buttercream seals the surface and helps the marzipan to adhere, the marzipan gives a wonderful flavor, and the fondant provides a perfectly smooth and shiny surface for decorating.

Fondant should be stored in a cool place with an airtight cover. After several weeks it can lose some moisture, which is why I recommend covering it with a thin layer of water to prevent dry hard spots from forming on the surface.

Covering a Cake with Marzipan

Place the filled cake on a sturdy cardboard circle. Cover the surface and sides of the cake with a thin layer of buttercream. Roll out a sheet of marzipan about 1/16 inch (2 mm) thick and 15 inches (38 cm) square for a 10-inch (25-cm) cake or 20 inches (50 cm) square for a 12-inch (30-cm) cake. Drape the marzipan over the cake and, with your hands, gently smooth the marzipan over the top and down the sides to eliminate any air bubbles or pleats. Using a sharp knife, trim any excess marzipan from around the bottom, keeping the marzipan flush with the cardboard round.

Glazing a Cake with Apricot

Although optional, I suggest that before applying the fondant, you brush the marzipan-covered cake with a thin coating of apricot glaze. Aside from adding a delicious taste, the glaze will gel and provide a very smooth foundation for the fondant. To make the glaze, heat a jar of apricot preserves with a little water to thin it and some sugar, stirring constantly, until the preserves are melted and smooth. While it is still hot, strain the syrup to remove any pieces of fruit. Spread the hot glaze over the marzipan using a soft pastry brush. Allow the glaze to cool and dry before pouring on the fondant. The pectin in the apricots will set up to form a skin, and the acidity in the fruit will prevent the sugar in the fondant from crystallizing.

Icing a Cake with Fondant

Fondant must be heated and thinned with simple syrup to make it pourable. Simple syrup is used instead of water because it increases the sugar solids content and maintains the fondant's high sheen. To make simple syrup, combine equal weights of sugar and water in a pot and heat until it reaches a full boil, stirring constantly. Cool the syrup before using. It will keep for months in the refrigerator, stored in a covered jar.

To melt the fondant, place it in the top of a double boiler set over hot water over low heat. Add a little simple syrup and half an egg white (the albumin in the egg white will have a drying effect after the fondant is poured). Stirring constantly, heat the fondant until it reaches 90°–95°F (30°–35°C), or about body temperature. Dilute the warm fondant with additional simple syrup until it is the proper consistency, about the thickness of buttermilk. If it is too thin, add more fondant. If it is too thick, add more simple syrup. Add food color if you wish. It is very important that the fondant not be overheated and that it be at the right temperature and viscosity before it is poured. You can test a small spoonful with your lips.

Before pouring the fondant over the cake, elevate the cake by placing it on a sturdy can (like a coffee can) over a sheet pan or baking tray covered with a cooling rack or wire grid. This will allow the fondant to drip down without collecting at the base of the cake and making a mess. The excess fondant can be scraped off and used again.

Pour the warm fondant onto the center of the cake. With a thin metal spatula, spread the fondant across the top and over the sides, using two or three motions. Scrape off any excess drippings with the spatula. As soon as the cake is iced and before it has set, place it on the serving plate or display platter. If you delay, the fondant will start to form small cracks when you move it. Let it dry completely before decorating the cake.

Note: When dipping small cakes or petits fours, adjust the thickness of the fondant. The smaller the surface area to be covered, the thinner the fondant; otherwise the fondant will be too viscous and sweet.

CAKES

These 12-inch (30-cm) decorated cakes were placed on 20-inch (50-cm) round pieces of plywood ½ inch (1.2 cm) thick that were covered with a coordinating color of soft royal icing, which was allowed to dry completely before the cakes were positioned. These platters are attractive for display. For real service, it may be more practical to use a metal or glass cake plate or stand.

Marzipan Cake—Modern Design (Fig. 8-1)

Cover a 12-inch (30-cm) cake with marzipan and ice it with cream-colored fondant. To make the flower design, draw a circle about half the diameter of the cake on a piece of cardboard with a pencil. For example, make a 6-inch (15-cm) circle for a 12-inch (30-cm) cake. Divide the circle into eight pieces (like a pie). Roll out a piece of dark plastic chocolate and cut out eight strips, each about ½ inch (1.2 cm) wide and approximately 7½ inches (19 cm) long. Loop each strip within the outline of each pie-shaped wedge. Place the assembled loops on the cake surface (be sure that the fondant is dry). Place a small orange marzipan disk inside each loop.

8-1

Make a small paper cone and fill it with white soft royal icing. Pipe a thin line on top of each loop and a small knob in the center of each orange disk. In the center of the flower place a small ball of marzipan dipped in egg white and rolled in coarse granulated sugar. The ball could be sprayed with yellow food color.

Make six small chocolate-colored marzipan balls and place them on both sides of the flower. To make the leaves and stem, roll out a thin sheet of green marzipan and roll it with a ribbed roller to make decorative lines. Roll a sheet of plastic chocolate to the same thickness with a plain roller. Cut out ovals with a metal cutter from the marzipan and plastic chocolate, and with a knife, cut each oval in half. Join half a marzipan oval and half a plastic chocolate circle to form each leaf. Decorate the rest of the cake with lines of white royal icing and melted chocolate piped out through a paper cone. Make the border with plastic chocolate surrounded with a ribbed ribbon of green marzipan. Surround the ribbon with a cord rolled from a piece of orange marzipan.

This cake was placed on a 20-inch (50-cm) round of plywood covered with soft yellow royal icing and decorated with chocolate and white royal icing.

Marzipan Cake with Fantasia Flowers (Fig. 8-2)

Cover a 12-inch (30-cm) cake with marzipan. Ice it with chocolate-colored fondant (add melted chocolate and a few drops of red food color to the melted fondant). Cover a 20-inch (50-cm) round piece of plywood with the same color chocolate soft royal icing.

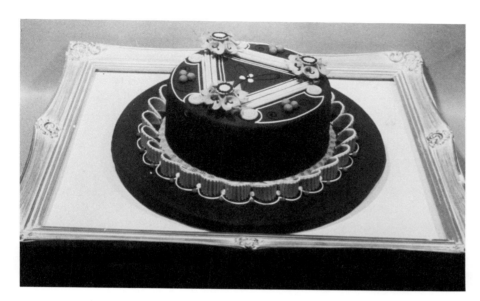

8-2

Place the cake in the center of the board. For decoration, roll out a piece of yellow marzipan and roll it again with a ribbed roller for decoration. Cut three strips approximately 8 inches (20 cm) long and 1½ inches (4 cm) wide. Place the three strips on the cake to make a triangle. Roll a piece of pastel green marzipan into a cord and place it on the outside of each strip, making a spiral curl at both ends. Place a flower on each of the three corners of the triangle. Each flower has five petals.

To make the flowers, roll a small piece of yellow marzipan approximately ⅟₁₆ inch (2 mm) thick. Using a plain round cutter, cut out fifteen ¾-inch (2-cm) circles. Use the same technique as for making rose petals (see page 84) using a flexible plastic scraper. With a sharp knife, cut a small triangle out of the tip of each petal. Pinch the broad side of the petal with two fingers, making a small cup. Let each petal dry a few hours before you assemble the five petals with soft royal icing. Cut three 1-inch (2.5-cm) circles out of orange marzipan and place them in the center of each flower. Spray the flowers with light orange food color. Place one flower on the three corners of the large triangle. Make nine ½-inch (1.2-cm) orange balls and place them on each side of the triangle as the picture shows.

For finishing, pipe white royal icing and chocolate lines with a paper cone on the cake and on the flowers. For the border, roll a piece of orange marzipan into a cord by hand and wrap it around the base of the cake. Place indentations on the cord using a modeling tool or plastic spoon.

Roll out a piece of light-green marzipan, roll it again with a ribbed roller, and cut out plain circles about 2 inches (5 cm) in diameter. Cut each circle in half. Bend the circles slightly and place them upright around the orange marzipan cord. Using a paper cone filled with white soft royal icing, pipe a line on top and in front of each bent circle. Place ¼-inch (6-cm) orange marzipan balls between each green loop around the border.

Marzipan Dome-Shaped Cake (Fig. 8-3)

Cover a 12-inch (30-cm) dome-shaped cake with marzipan and ice it with a pastel yellow-green fondant. For decoration, roll out a piece of yellow-green marzipan. Cut four strips ¾ inch (2 cm) wide and make rings by wrapping them around a metal cutter or a small round jar that is approximately 3½ inches (9 cm) in diameter. Arrange the rings on the fondant (see picture). Make a large double marzipan rose out of yellow marzipan (see page 84–86 for instructions). I tinted the first layer of petals light yellow, and the outer layers gradually darker for contrast. Before shaping and assembling the petals, I rolled them with a ribbed roller to give them some texture.

8-3

116

To finish, roll out a small piece of plastic chocolate and place a half circle on the marzipan ring. Using a paper cone, pipe a thin line of royal icing for decoration. Make the stems from plastic chocolate. With a paper cone, pipe a few simple lines of melted chocolate for finishing. Make the border from a strip of light-green marzipan rolled with a ribbed roller.

Marzipan Cake "Cora" (Fig. 8-4)

Cover a 12-inch (30-cm) cake with marzipan and ice it with pastel yellow fondant. Place the cake on a 20-inch (50-cm) round of plywood ½ inch (1.2 cm) thick. Cover the plywood with the same color soft royal icing.

Make a bouquet of nine red marzipan roses placed on a few plastic chocolate stems. Surround the roses with two-tone green and chocolate-colored marzipan leaves (see Chapter 5 for instructions).

The name "Cora" (my wife's) is made from plastic chocolate. To make the letters, roll a thin ribbon of plastic chocolate, cut it to form the letters, and place the letters standing up. Using a paper cone, pipe a thin white line of soft royal icing on top for contrast.

To make the border, surround the cake with a marzipan ribbon rolled with a ribbed roller. Cut small hearts out of red marzipan and stick them into the fondant above the ribbon.

8-4

MARZIPAN COOKIES (Fig. 8-5 a-c)

Marzipan cookies are produced weekly in fine European pastry shops. They are a way of showing your culinary "business card" in your display window. It would seem to be a time-consuming task, but like anything else, making large trays with a wide assortment eventually becomes routine. I was always surprised at what I was able to produce with only a few apprentices to help.

These small decorated almond macaroons are usually sold by weight or by the piece. Each decorated cookie weighs approximately ½ ounce (14 grams) and is shaped into a small round or rectangle. The marzipan figures are placed on top, attached with a little melted cocoa butter. Most of the marzipan figures shown on the cookies are described in the opening chapters. Don't be limited, however, by my suggestions—use your imagination to come up with other ideas.

ALMOND MACAROONS

1 pound (448 grams) almond paste
½ pound (224 grams) granulated sugar
½ pound (224 grams) powdered sugar
6 egg whites
1 teaspoon grated lemon peel

---

1. Combine the almond paste, granulated sugar, and powdered sugar in a mixing bowl. With the mixer running, slowly add the egg whites. Blend the mixture together together, scraping the sides of the bowl occasionally, until the mixture is smooth and lump-free.

2. Place the dough in a pastry bag fitted with a ½-inch (1.2-cm) round plain tip. Squeeze small cookies onto a parchment- or waxed paper–lined baking sheet.

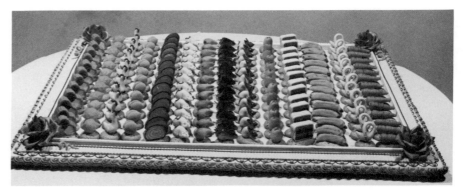

8-5a

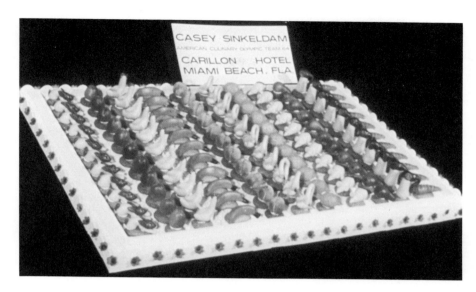

8-5b

2. Flatten the surface of each macaroon with a damp towel.
3. Bake in a preheated 325°F oven for 10–12 minutes. Remove from the oven. If the macaroons stick to the paper, lay the paper on top of a damp towel and then release them with a metal spatula.

I will explain how each cookie is made, from left to right.

Row 1. This tricolor cookie is formed by stacking three marzipan logs, white, pink, and chocolate, into a triangle with the chocolate log on top. The logs are covered with a sheet of light orange marzipan rolled with a ribbed roller. Each cookie is sliced with a sharp knife, about ½ inch (1.2 cm) thick.

Rows 2, 3, and 4. A lemon, a chicken, and a peach, all formed out of marzipan, are attached to round macaroons with a little melted cocoa butter. The chicken is made as follows: Make a ball, and then a pear, elongating the broad end to form the chicken's neck, the stem end to form the tail. With a sharp modeling tool make an indentation for the feathers. Pipe on soft royal icing for the beak and head feathers.

Row 5. To make this swirled cookie, place a sheet of pink marzipan over a sheet of white marzipan and roll them into a log, about ¾ inch (2 cm) thick. Wrap the log with a thin sheet of chocolate-colored marzipan. Cut the bar with a sharp knife into ½-inch (1.2-cm) slices and place them on the cookies.

119

Rows 6 through 10.   Marzipan figures of white mice, pears, strawberries, rabbits, and apples are attached to cookies with a little melted cocoa butter. To make a mouse, make a ball and then a short sausage, tapering one end to a point to form the snout. Flatten the bottom of the sausage against the work surface so that it lies flat. Make a very thin cord out of marzipan and attach it to the rump, curling it up over the back. Make two ears. With a modeling tool make two indentations to show the hips. With soft royal icing, pipe out the eyes.

Row 11.   This layered bar is made from chocolate- and orange-colored sheets of marzipan placed on top of each other. Cover the bar with a thin layer of white marzipan and cut into ½-inch (1.2-cm) slices with a sharp knife.

Rows 12 through 15.   Attach marzipan bananas, little white swans, and carrots with melted cocoa butter to the cookies. To make a swan, first make a ball in a pointy pear shape. As for a chicken, elongate the broad end into a long neck. Bend the neck into a horseshoe shape. With a sharp tool, make indentations for feathers and eyes. Place a small beak on the neck. Using orange marzipan, make a small horseshoe for the legs. Place the body on top of the legs and pipe in the eyeballs with soft royal icing.

A very effective way of displaying these cookies is to place them on a tray covered and decorated with pastillage. Figure 8-5c shows one I made for a children's party. Notice that one of the marzipan clowns is standing on his finger in total balance!

8-5c

SHOWPIECES AND DISPLAYS

In my career I have made and displayed many successful showpieces. Most often I used various combinations of marzipan, pastillage, plastic chocolate, and royal icing because I love working with these different textures. The examples in this chapter (all found in the color insert) are representative of projects made using these four components. Having made so many over the years, I have had the opportunity to work with different formulations for them, to increase my understanding about how ingredients behave, and to expand my knowledge about techniques for many different applications.

ORGANIZING YOUR THOUGHTS

Creating large-scale displays and interesting showpieces is a fantastic opportunity for showing your professional talent. It requires a lot of organization and planning—the larger the display, the more work you should do in advance. Before you start a project, put your thoughts on paper. What is its purpose? Will your display tell a story or describe an activity—either real or fantasized? What will the color combinations be? How big is it? How difficult will the project be to execute? I like incorporating a humorous aspect in my showpieces, but whatever you choose, I advise that you stay away from anything that could be offensive to others, be it political or religious. In addition, the content of your display must be absolutely respectable and honorable.

After you have done the preliminary planning, make a tentative layout with the proposed dimensions. When you are satisfied with the layout and proportions, make a paper model. I use thin cardboard and paper. The model will give you a better idea of what the project will look like and at the same time allow you to make changes at no cost until you are satisfied.

It is never too early to start thinking about how you are going to pack and ship your display if you are planning on sending it somewhere, to a food show or to a client's home, for example. Don't wait until the last minute to do this research, or you will inevitably spend more time and money to compensate for your poor planning. Even the most seemingly straightforward considerations are often overlooked: Is the trunk of your car big enough or do you need to borrrow one that is? If your display piece is large, will you be able to get it through the door frames, both where it is being built and where it will be displayed? If the answer is no, you may have to consider planning the piece in such a way that it can be easily disassembled and reassembled in sections; otherwise it will be like building a boat in the basement that you are unable to move outside. Chapter 10 contains additional suggestions about packing and shipping.

LARGE-SCALE SHOWPIECES

The Kitchen (Fig. C4)

My favorite showpiece has always been the kitchen, because it is a display that tells a story. It is about an everyday experience, which makes it realistic and full of action. I try to build a story into all my displays—the results are much more interesting than just portraying a static scene.

The display details a moment in a busy hotel kitchen. The sous-chef holding a fork is in the process of dishing up the main course of beef Wellington, while his assistant removes a copper stockpot from the stove. In the background are several apprentices putting away crates of fruits and vegetables. The sous-chef needs more dishes and his student is ready to give them to him, when ooops!—the poor fellow trips over two crates of peaches and starts to slide while carrying a stack of dinner plates. (I see the plates falling, and from past experience know the feeling . . . .) Meanwhile, the executive chef, who is figuring out his food costs in his office off the kitchen, hears the commotion and jumps up to see what has happened. Over in the pastry department, the pastry chef is about to put the final decorations on a wedding cake. You can tell from the expression on her face that she knows what has just happened. Behind her a baker is preparing Danish pastries for the coffee shop, and the breadbaker is removing French breadsticks from the old-fashioned brick oven. In the corner two sheet pans of cookies have been removed from an electric oven to cool.

The kitchen is a very complex piece with a lot of action; I love including a lot of detail, although admittedly you must have a lot of patience. Perhaps you will be inspired to create an equally complex set.

The kitchen was mounted on a base and floor made of plywood and Styrofoam. The entire contents, however, were made completely from marzipan, royal icing, and pastillage. The basic dimensions are as follows:

> Plywood base: 34 inches (85 cm) long
> 19 inches (48 cm) wide
> ¾ inch (2 cm) thick
> Kitchen walls: 30 inches (75 cm) long
> 15 inches (38 cm) wide
> 10 inches (25 cm) high
> The kitchen floor was placed on a sheet of Styrofoam:
> 30 inches (75 cm) long
> 15 inches (38 cm) wide
> 1 inch (2.5 cm) thick

I cut the Styrofoam at a slight angle to create a three-dimensional appearance, and covered it with a ¼-inch (6-mm) sheet of pastillage, using soft royal icing as a glue, which I completely spread over the Styrofoam with a thin metal spatula. When the pastillage was dry, I sanded it until it was smooth. The floor tiles were made from ¾-inch (2-cm) squares of yellow and brown marzipan, which I arranged in a checkerboard grid using soft royal icing as a glue. I used about 800 tiles in all.

The worktables, shelves, office desk, refrigerator, electric oven, and mixing machine were made from pastillage tinted light yellow. Each worktable is different in shape and size, but they are all 2¼ inches (5.75 cm) high. Every tabletop is covered with a ½ inch (1.2 cm) larger wooden-colored surface, approximately ½ inch (1.2 cm) thick (Fig. C5). To make the wooden grain on the tables, I diluted a thick coffee or carmel syrup with alcohol (whiskey, gin, or vodka) and applied a thin coat of it using a soft brush. I then dragged a dry fan brush (a small stiff painter's brush with bristles in a flat fan shape) back and forth in one direction to create the grainy texture.

The sous-chef's table (Fig. C5) contains a large tray of sliced beef Wellington, mashed potatoes, green peas, cauliflower, and carrots. All the food was modeled with marzipan, except for the mashed potatoes, which were piped out with royal icing. The dishes were all made from pastillage and are ¾ inch (2 cm) round.

The executive chef's office (Fig. C6) contains his desk, on top of which lies open his slightly curled desk pad. The student's stack of plates (Figs. C7 and C8) was made from pastillage, as was the stockpot behind him. Figures C9 and C10 show the sous-chef and the assistant in greater detail. Figures C11 and C12 are close-ups of the crates filled with vegetables and fruit and a dish with tomatoes. All the food was made from marzipan. The crates were made from pastillage, which was textured and slightly marbleized with color to simulate wood. Notice the nails at the corners. I placed a quarter and a peach in each picture to give you an idea of the scale and dimensions. Figure C13 shows the pastry chef in front of her five-tier wedding cake. Each layer is decorated with a lot of detail—even the icing dripping from the tip of her pastry bag is included.

Park Scene (Fig. C14)

When I made this centerpiece, I was thinking about a sunny Sunday afternoon, many years ago, when my family went for a stroll in the park. It was a special treat for us, and usually included an ice cream or some candy. As we walked, we heard music in the distance, and coming closer, we saw it was from a group of musicians. Listening to the music was a romantic couple sitting on a bench being photographed. The scene was idyllic, with a swan gliding past in a small pond nearby.

This scene is another example of a moment captured from real life. It shows a lot of action—the musicians playing their instruments, the photographer focusing his camera, the couple thinking of a kiss. Look at your daily activities to find ideas for creating another story to tell.

The centerpiece was mounted on an oval plywood base, 4 feet (120 cm) long, 20 inches (50 cm) wide, and ½ inch (1.2 cm) thick. The base was covered with light yellow-brown soft royal icing. The figures were made from marzipan; the music grandstand from pastillage; and the trees, shrubs, and flowers from marzipan decorated with royal icing.

"We Don't Like Monkey Business" Centerpiece (Fig. C15)

I titled this piece "We Don't Like Monkey Business" because it is a sentiment that I believe in and practice. However, that doesn't mean that I can't have some fun modeling it. You could use this idea to group other animals or figures on a rock or mountain formation.

The piece was mounted on a round plywood base 24 inches (60 cm) in diameter. The rocks and platforms that the monkeys are standing on were made from pieces of Styrofoam and clean empty cans and boxes that I stacked and grouped together. I dipped pieces of soft cloth in pastel yellow soft royal icing, and while they were still wet, draped the fabric over the Styrofoam-can frame, bunching the cloth together and making pleats and creases to simulate rock formations. When the cloth was completely dry after several days, I used a spray gun to apply several shades of contrasting food colors to give the arrangement more depth. For the waterfall I placed a few thin dry pieces of pastillage against the rock and piped light blue soft royal icing from the top down. The monkey figures were made from marzipan.

SMALLER DISPLAYS

Marzipan Cold Cuts (Fig. C16)

This showpiece is a good way to demonstrate your talents at making realistic-looking food out of marzipan. Although the piece itself is not very practical (although you could certainly enter it in a food show), the techniques for forming the meats and cheese are useful to know should you need to make marzipan food as a component of another display.

It is important to understand how to color the marzipan in order to make the cold cuts look authentic. You will need to do a lot of blending to get the colors right. The best way is to buy a fresh assortment of the real things (in this case, sausages, corned beef, roast beef, ham, and Swiss and American cheeses) and copy the colors. Tint small pieces of marzipan at a time, so as not to waste a lot if you get the color wrong. Keep in mind that the colors should look appetizing as well as realistic.

Besides standard food colors, cocoa powder mixed with corn syrup and a few drops of red food color is a good way to tint many of the meats. Smoked meats and sausages are usually ruddier or browner red than fresh meats.

125

Notice that some sausages have thick skin, others have thin, and all contain fat, which can be simulated by rolling in pieces of white marzipan, as described below.

To make a fresh liver sausage, roll out a sheet of marzipan, tinted a reddish-brown, about ¼ inch (6 mm) thick. Make thin bars of white marzipan, also about ¼ inch (6 mm) thick, and as long as the marzipan sheet. These will be the fat within the sausage. Lay the white bars lengthwise over the sheet. Make sure that the bars are arranged with spaces in between, otherwise you will end up with giant white chunks, instead of small streaks, of "fat." Roll up the sheet like a jelly roll, pushing and pressing out the air as you roll. To make the skin of the sausage, roll out of a sheet of white marzipan—the thickness to be determined by the type of sausage you are making. Tightly wrap the sausage log in the skin.

A smoked sausage, ham, or other meat will generally have a more variegated color tone. To get this effect, you must marbleize several shades of marzipan before you roll it up into a log or shape it into a roast. Take several pieces of tinted marzipan (a ham, for example, would contain pink, darker pink, and light brown shades), and roughly cut the pieces into ¼-inch (6-mm) cubes. Knead the cubes together, folding and blending, but being careful not to completely amalgamate the colors. Shape the marzipan as desired, and brush the surface with a mixture of red and brown food colors diluted with alcohol to give it a roasted or smoked appearance.

To make Swiss cheese, tint a block of marzipan the same yellow color as Swiss cheese. To make the holes, push a thin wooden dowel all the way through in several places. Brush the outside of the block with light brown food color for the rind.

Let the marzipan foods dry for several hours before cutting. The inside of the marzipan will still be slightly soft, so be careful not to squash it. Cut the slices with a long sharp knife, using a long back-and-forth motion. Lay the slices on a tray. In Figure C16, I covered and decorated a piece of plywood with pastillage and accented it with a marzipan pig's head and a cow at the corners.

Pastillage Delft-Blue Plate Setting (Figs. C17 and C18)

I have a small collection of Delft-blue dishes that I replicated in pastillage and then painted. The technique can be used for creating any kind of dish in pastillage. The key to success is to be absolutely sure that the pastillage is the same thickness for all the dishes. To do this, first knead a piece of pastillage until it is completely smooth. Roll it out with a rolling pin until it is slightly flattened. You may need to use a little powdered sugar to keep it from sticking to the work surface. Take two metal or wooden dowels [for these dishes the dowels were ⅟₁₆ inch (2 mm) in diameter] and place the rods on each side of the pastillage. Place the rolling pin on top of the rods and roll the pastillage until the pin rests evenly on the rods. The pastillage sheet will be completely even with the rods.

Take the pastillage sheet and place it over a real plate, saucer, or cup dusted with powdered sugar, pressing it to smooth. Remove any excess with a sharp knife. Let the pastillage dry at room temperature for one or two days before you remove it from the model. It will come off easily. Sand the plates with fine sandpaper until they are very smooth, and remove any powder dust with a soft brush. With a clean damp cloth, quickly wipe each plate to remove any fine crystals before you start painting.

With a pencil, draw a picture or design on the plate. Keep in mind the main thing you want to show and make that your focus. For example, notice in the large plate in Figure C17 that the horse and buggy are surrounded with white, empty space—not cluttered with detail that would distract the eye. When I was ready to paint, I placed blue food color in several small cups and diluted it with varying amounts of alcohol to control the shade.

Figure C18 shows several of the dishes on a handpainted doily piped out using royal icing on a round piece of plywood covered with chocolate-colored royal icing. (See the next example for how to make the doily.)

Candy Dishes and Doilies (Fig. C19)

These candy dishes were made from pastel-colored pastillage, which was rolled out between two bars to ensure an even thickness (see the description for the Delft-blue dishes for this technique). Each dish was covered and decorated with marzipan and plastic chocolate. The dishes were placed on pastillage circles, 12 inches (30 cm) in diameter, which were piped over with a doily design made out of soft royal icing.

To create the doily, lightly trace a real doily onto the pastillage surface with a pencil. Make a small paper cone and clip off the end to form the tip. Fill the cone with the icing and hold it about 2 inches (5 cm) above the drawing. Let the icing fall in place, applying even pressure on the cone. Try to make it elegant looking with many details. It takes a lot of time and patience to do this, but it is a good exercise in control.

John F. Kennedy Mosaic (Fig. C20 and C21)

I created this portrait of President Kennedy for a political conference in a hotel where I was working. To make it challenging, I tried a new technique, which you could use for your own creations. The portrait is a mosaic of colored pastillage tiles, which were glued together with royal icing "grout" and framed with dark plastic chocolate.

Make the base out of a piece of plywood [this portrait was 16 x 20 inches (40 × 50 cm)], spread it with soft royal icing, and cover it with a thin sheet of pastillage, smoothed out to eliminate any air bubbles. Draw the outline of the portrait (or whatever your design is) onto the pastillage with pencil. If you do not feel artistically competent to do this freehand, enlarge or blow-up a photograph or picture and then trace it onto the pastillage. If you have a slide projector, you can take a slide of the image and project it onto the surface of your showpiece for tracing. Or, if you have an overhead projector, place the picture underneath and trace from the projected image.

To plan the tiles, make a list of the colors you want to use. The easiest way to do this is to make a rough drawing and fill it in with colored pencils. It will give you a better idea about proportions and color combinations. When you are satisfied with this "draft," start making the pastillage tiles.

Tint the pastillage the appropriate colors and roll each piece between two rods or bars until it is $\frac{1}{16}$ inch (2 mm) thick (see page 127 for instructions on how to do this). Let each sheet dry flat on a wooden surface. (Wood is preferable to a stainless steel or any other nonporous surface because wood absorbs moisture, allowing the pastillage to dry evenly on both sides.) Let it dry for at least 24 hours, and then break the pastillage into small pieces. Arrange the pastillage chips over the pastillage base, gluing them down with soft royal icing (Fig. C21). Try to put the pieces close together, but leave a little space in between each chip. When the mosaic is completely covered and finished, let it dry for at least one day.

Pour soft royal icing over the whole picture, filling in the cavities between each tile with a scraper or thin metal spatula. Immediately remove any excess icing before it sets. When it is completely dry, sand the surface with fine sandpaper until it is smooth. Remove any powder with a soft brush, and wipe the surface clean with a damp cloth. You can put the picture in a plastic chocolate or chocolate-colored marzipan frame if you wish.

C1

C2

C3

C4

C5

C6

C7

C8

C9

C10

C11

C12

C13

C14

C15

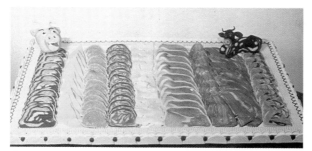

C16

C17

C18

C19

C20

C21

C22

C23

C24

C26

C25

C27

C28

C29A

C29B

C30

C31

C32

MASTERPIECES FROM A MASTER
(Figs. C22–C26)

Before I came to America many years ago, I met Mr. Jan Weetink at the awards ceremony of a culinary arts show in Amsterdam. Jan, who is older than I am and retired now, is a master of pulled sugar art and often used combinations of pulled sugar, pastillage, plastic chocolate, marzipan, and royal icing in his showpieces. Over the years we have kept in touch, and to this day—more than 30 years later—we still challenge each other with new ideas and techniques. I asked him for permission to show some of his many talents in this book, because I think his art can be an inspiration and model for others. It is my great pleasure and honor to show you five of his very special masterpieces.

Plastic Chocolate Pipe Organ (Fig. C22)

This fantastic piece is a model of an old-fashioned pipe organ from one of the large churches in Amsterdam, made from pastillage and three kinds of plastic chocolate: white, milk, and dark. The organ base and pipes are made from pastillage, every pipe individually formed and then covered with a thin layer of white plastic chocolate. To marbleize the plastic chocolate, as was done on the pipes, cut dark, milk, and white plastic chocolate into several ¼-inch (6-mm) pieces and toss them together to evenly distribute the colors. Knead them together, but do not completely blend them. Roll the mass out into a thin sheet, and rub it with the palm of your hand until it is shiny. Coat the pastillage with a very thin layer of soft royal icing using a brush or flexible metal spatula before you cover it with the plastic chocolate.

Each statue on the organ was sculpted freehand using combinations of the three kinds of plastic chocolate, as was the crest of the city of Amsterdam. The group of choral singers and the director at the base were made from white chocolate only. The singers are mounted on a platform, and in the background is a vase filled with white chocolate flowers. In total, a beautiful showpiece with elaborate detail.

Candy Dishes (Figs. C23 and C24)

These candy dishes are made from pastillage, each one different and beautifully decorated. One even contains white chocolate truffles. The technique for

129

forming the dishes is the same as for the Delft-blue dishes: a sheet of pastill-age is pressed over a model and left to dry before the model is removed (see pages 126–127 for additional details). The pastillage on several of the dishes was rolled with ribbed rolling pins and decoratively scored before it was molded. All the flowers, leaves, and butterflies were made from white plastic chocolate, which was tinted in a pleasant harmony of pastel shades. Marzipan was used for some of the finishing and border work.

The crackled or cracked surface on several of the lids was made by a special technique. Roll out a piece of pastillage on a stainless steel or other nonporous surface, but not on wood. (The reason for not using wood in this case, unlike when drying pastillage for making mosaic tiles, is that you want the top side of the pastillage to dry and the bottom side to remain moist. A surface such as stainless steel prevents the side in contact with it from drying as fast as the exposed top.) After one or two hours, a crust will start to form. At this stage, slide your hand underneath the pastillage and move your fingers gently, making large and small cracks on the crusted surface. Remove your hand and roll the surface of the pastillage with a small rolling pin. The cracks will open. Fill the cracks with soft royal icing in a contrasting color. Immedi-ately remove any excess before it dries, and place the pastillage over the dish or dish lid, dusted with powdered sugar. When the surface of the pastillage has a slight thin crust, sand it smooth with fine sandpaper and clean off the powder with a damp cloth.

Flower Arrangement (Fig. C25)

This flower arrangement is made completely from white chocolate. By blend-ing and mixing different shades and colors of the plastic chocolate, you can simulate a streaking effect in the large leaves and in the driftwood piece in the center (see instructions on how to streak or marbleize on pages 88 and 126). The flowers and the large leaves were formed over a thin metal wire frame for strength and support.

The base of this floral arrangement is a round piece of styrofoam covered with white plastic chocolate. The small candy dishes surrounding the flower centerpiece make a beautiful grouping. Look closely at the details and decora-tions on the covers of the candy dishes. The plastic chocolate butterflies look like they are ready to fly away.

The Heron (Fig. C26)

This beautiful water-loving bird was made from blown sugar covered with a thin layer of plastic chocolate. Blown sugar makes a good base, providing the sugar is protected with the plastic chocolate. (The chocolate protects the sugar from moisture.) Each feather was made out of plastic chocolate and placed individually. The colors are mainly white with some milk chocolate for the tail. An alternative way of forming this bird would be to make it out of pastillage. A steel wire must be placed inside the pastillage to support the neck and legs.

The three water lilies, made out of white plastic chocolate, were placed on a light blue pastillage base, which was crackled and painted blue to simulate water. To get this effect, roll out a sheet of pastillage on a smooth surface. Paint the pastillage blue. (Make sure the blue, or whatever color you chose, is diluted with alcohol so that it evaporates quickly. You can speed up the process by blowing the surface dry with a hair dryer.) A crust will soon form. Slide your hand underneath and move your fingers to form cracks. Roll a small rolling pin back and forth over the surface a few times to open the cracks more. The white will contrast with the painted surface. Place the pastillage sheet on the base to dry before you place the bird and water lilies on top.

TALENT FROM A STUDENT (Figs. C27–C32)

Now that I have shown you masterpieces from a master, I will include some pieces that were made by a student, who happens to be my daughter Patricia Lynn. These pieces are good examples of work that can be done by someone without years and years of experience, but who is creative and skilled.

Decorated Cake (Fig. C27)

This cake was covered with a thin layer of marzipan and iced with cream-colored fondant. When the fondant dried, six light-green marzipan rings were arranged in a circle on top of the cake. Each ring was finished with another ring of chocolate marzipan and decorated in the center with marzipan. A double marzipan rose was placed in the center with a few marzipan leaves. The cake was placed on a glass circle painted black. (Patty used regular paint for this and let the glass dry for several weeks so that any odor would dissipate.)

Raisin Lunch Box (Fig. C28)

The inspiration for this lunch box came from those popular raisin figures created for the California Raisin Board. Patty spent a lot of time mixing the right colors and modeling them to match the real thing. She used a stainless steel wire to support the arms and legs, which she then covered with marzipan. The sandwich, two pieces of white bread and several slices of cold cuts, was made entirely from marzipan also. On the side of the sandwich are a marzipan apple and banana. The lunch box itself was made from light yellow pastillage.

Funny Creatures (Figs. C29 a&b, C30, C31, C32)

On a family trip Patty bought some unusual plastic figurines she saw in a store window. She later modeled them in marzipan and used them for a cake decoration. The three creatures are all holding a "crystal" from an open treasure box. My wife thinks Patty's work is better than mine. Well done, Patty!

CHAPTER 1

PACKING AND SHIPPING

LONG-DISTANCE MOVES

If you need to ship your marzipan, pastillage, or chocolate constructions, you can save yourself hours of repair work at their destination if you pack your display pieces properly at the beginning. Marzipan is fragile and must be treated with great care for shipment. I believe that at least 25 percent of your total time working on a display must be spent protecting it. That may seem like a lot, but in the end that investment saves time, money, aggravation, and disappointment. If you know how to pack your work safely, you can take advantage of opportunities to send your work far from home—not only to food shows, but to customers who don't live locally.

I sent the kitchen showpiece (pages 122–124) from my home in North Carolina to a culinary food show in Frankfurt, Germany, where it survived truck transport, three planes, and several weeks of storage in an airport warehouse with no damage whatsoever. I was completely sure that nothing would go wrong because I knew that I had packed it securely. Let me describe how I did this.

Every figure, table, partition, crate, dish—everything—was placed in a specially designed box to fit that particular piece only. I measured every unit, added 2 inches (5 cm) extra, and made stiff cardboard boxes that I then covered on the inside with 1-inch (2.5-cm) thick foam rubber (Fig. 10-1). I filled any empty spaces with small pieces of foam rubber, tissue paper, and

133

other soft packing materials so the contents would remain stationary. I then packed all these smaller boxes inside larger ones (Fig. 10-2), which were also covered on the inside with foam rubber.

I packed all these larger boxes inside a foam rubber-lined 2-inch (5-cm) thick plywood crate, with reinforced sides and corners (Fig. 10-3). Inside this crate I built an adjustable shelf in the center to evenly distribute the weight of the boxes. I did this by screwing two adjustable shelving standards (strips) into each of the long walls of the crate. The shelf was supported with hooks. Once the boxes were distributed inside the crate and all spaces between the boxes were stuffed tightly, I screwed the whole thing shut. Nothing could possibly shift or move during the long transport that lay ahead, and nothing did.

SHORT-DISTANCE MOVES

If you are moving a construction by yourself by truck or car, it is not necessary to make as elaborate precautions as I did for the transcontinental move I just described. Since you will not be turning your work over to others for transport, the boxes do not need to be as securely packed as for sending the same material by plane. Depending upon the size of your car or truck, you could pump a child's inflatable swimming pool or a large inner tube half full with air and place the boxes in that. The swimming pool or tube will absorb shocks and vibrations. A thick layer of foam rubber also gives a smooth ride. Just make sure the boxes cannot slide during transport.

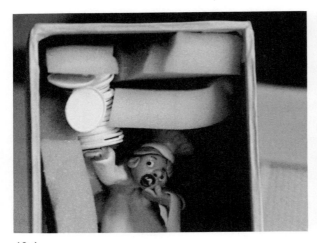

10-1

10-2

134

10-3

When packing small ornaments, such as marzipan flowers or fragile pieces of pastillage, place them individually in small boxes, such as match boxes, and fill any empty spaces with soft tissue paper. When you shake the box, you should hear nothing. Place these boxes inside a larger box, also stuffed with paper, soft cloth, or foam rubber, so that the smaller boxes remain stationary.

WITHIN A BUILDING

Transporting something delicate, like a marzipan fruit centerpiece or a four- or five-layer wedding cake, from the pastry shop to the function room in a hotel is not always as easy as it looks, even though you never have to leave the building. Often you have to go through the lobby, take an elevator, and go up a few steps to get where you are going.

Assuming the cake or marzipan centerpiece is too big to be carried easily, place it on a small cart or wagon with wheels. I recommend that you place a thick piece of foam rubber [2 to 5 inches (5 to 13 cm)] underneath each shelf of the cart to absorb any vibrations when going over uneven surfaces.

135

DROP TEST

When packing decorations in boxes, it is a good idea to test in advance whether your packing can withstand any movement, particularly if you are shipping your constructions by truck or airplane. Take each box and drop it from a height of 48 inches (120 cm) onto the floor. Roll the box over a few times, open it up, and evaluate the results. If nothing happened, you have done a good job. If the piece has been damaged, you must improve your packing method and try again. It's best to test your precautions in advance, rather than find out you have a problem at the destination.

INDEX